Solid, Safe, Secure

BUILDING ARCHIVES
REPOSITORIES IN AUSTRALIA

TED LING

NATIONAL
ARCHIVES
OF AUSTRALIA

ISBN 0 642 34403 5

National Library of Australia Cataloguing-in-Publication entry:
Ling, Ted
Solid, Safe, Secure: Building Archives Repositories in Australia

Bibliography
Includes index
ISBN 0 642 34403 5

1. Archive buildings.
II. National Archives of Australia
II.Title
725.150994

Project Management: Stephen Hall Associates
Editors: Maggie Shapley and Susan Hall
Design: Art Direction **Layout:** Kristy Fransen
Printed by: Goanna Print

This book in a number of instances makes specific reference to particular products of manufacturers. Such products are quoted as a means of exemplification and the National Archives should not be seen to be endorsing any product or expressing any preference for one manufacturers product over another. The National Archives of Australia has taken every possible care in the preparation of the guidelines in this book. However, the Archives, its employees and agents accept no responsibility or liability in respect of any loss or damage however caused that may arise as a result of the provision of the guidelines or flowing from any of the advice or recommendations made pursuant to these guidelines.

Note: In 1998 Australian Archives (previously also Commonwealth Archives Office) changed its name to the National Archives of Australia.

'The only person who is competent to plan an archives building is one who has just completed the planning of one, and seen it erected and brought into use'

Robert Sharman, 1968

CONTENTS

Foreword

Archives buildings store and preserve the records we wish to keep for posterity. Buildings are the first line of defence in the defence in the preservation of valuable items of our heritage. Without adequate care much of our recorded heritage would never survive, but few people are aware of the skills and knowledge required in providing these buildings.

The National Archives of Australia has been constructing and managing archives buildings for more than 30 years. It is fitting that Ted Ling, Director of our Darwin office, has provided a book encapsulating the experience gained by the Archives and the lessons learned along the way.

Solid, Safe, Secure is a milestone. For the first time in this country all major aspects of design, construction and management of an archives building appear in the one publication. The book demystifies what can be a complex subject and at the same time conveys an appreciation that archives buildings are more than concrete, bricks and steel. This book, with its carefully selected illustrations, shows how to approach the goal of international best practice in design, materials and techniques for storage of previous records.

I am sure that this book will be valued by all archives organisations, both large and small.

George Nichols
Director-General
National Archives of Australia

Preface

This is a book about archival buildings. How they are designed, built and managed.

The book is written with the intention of providing a reference source for archivists, particularly those faced for the first time with coordinating the construction of a major facility on behalf of their archives. It addresses many issues and, while it does not pretend to provide all the answers, it does aim to tell you some of the matters of which you should be aware and the type of questions that you should be asking architects, engineers and builders.

As far as possible, the book has been written in plain English in order to promote a better understanding of what are, in reality, highly technical subjects. The author is an archivist – not an architect, engineer, draftsman or a builder – who spent six years with the National Archives' Facilities program.

The book is principally concerned with Australian archives buildings, for which comprehensive literature has been sadly lacking. While there are reference works which deal with buildings in North America or Europe, rarely do they give consideration to Australian buildings and environmental conditions. This is unfortunate as the book will show that Australian institutions have a wealth of knowledge and experience when it comes to constructing and operating archival buildings.

Last, the book is primarily intended for buildings meant to house permanent value records, rather than temporary value. The principles can, however, be readily be adapted to buildings which house temporary value records.

Acknowledgements

In writing this book I am aware that many staff from the National Archives and other organisations within Australia and overseas have provided me with advice, answered my queries, verified my sources, commented on the draft text and given me general support:

Peter Anderson, Chairman of the International Council on Archives' Committee on Buildings and Equipment and Deputy Keeper of the Scottish Record Office; Michel Duchein, Honaraire Inspecteur-General Technical Service des Archives, France; Christopher Kitching, Secretary of the Royal Commission on Historical Manuscripts, United Kingdom; Peter Pavel Klasinc, Director of the International Association of Archival Science; and George MacKenzie, Deputy Secretary-General, International Council on Archives. Also, Ian Batterham, Les Cargill, Veronica Chlap, Anne Cooke, John Crimmins, John de Salis, Brian Hay, Cheryl Jackson, Chris Lowger, Warwick Peberdy, Claire Sadler, Anne-Marie Schwirtlich, Kylie Scroope, Craig Stevens, Eileen Tannachion and Stephen Yorke.

My thanks also goes to all those who provided me with specific information, photographs and pertinent statistics about their facilities:

John Cross, Archives Office of New South Wales; Ross Gibbs, Michael Tinsley and Darryl O'Callaghan, Public Record Office of Victoria; Lee McGregor, Queensland State Archives; Ian Pearce, Archives Office of Tasmania; Helen Smith, BHP Pty Ltd; Helen McNaught, National Archives of New Zealand; Bruno Corre, Archives Territoriales, New Caledonia; Michele Pacifico, National Archives and Records Administration, United States of America; Terresa McIntosh, National Archives of Canada; Andrew McDonald, Public Record Office, United Kingdom; Wolf Buchmann, Bundesarchiv, Germany; Bjorn Lindh, Riksarkivet, Sweden; Leif Andressen, Riksarkivet, National Archives of Norway; Shen Lihua, State Archives Bureau of China; Koo Man-Seop, Government Archives and Records Service, Republic of Korea; Simon Chu and Sarah Choy, Public Records Office, Hong Kong; and Pitt Kuan Wah, National Archives of Singapore.

I would also like to record my special thanks to Barry Snodgrass, Director of the National Archives' Facilities program, for his guidance and support during the writing of this book. He also read and commented on the draft text and provided many suggestions for improvement.

And last, Michael Piggott from the National Archives who, by asking me to write an article on the development of archival buildings in Australia for publication in Archives and Manuscripts in 1994, unwittingly inspired my desire to preach the subject, a desire which remains as strong today as it was then.

Introduction

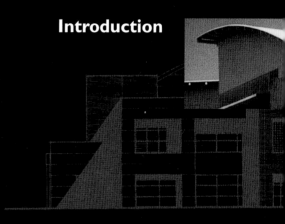

EAST E

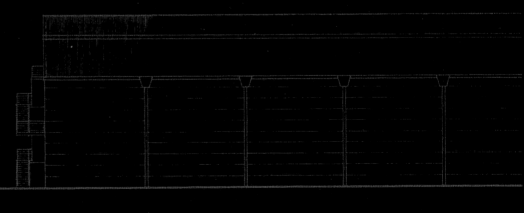

SOUTH

Archives Buildings

The preservation of valuable records – regardless of their physical format – owes much to the buildings in which they are housed.

The construction of archival facilities on a worldwide basis has never been more prominent than in the past decade. There have been new facilities completed or under way in the USA, Canada, England, Sweden, Australia, China, South Korea, Hong Kong and Singapore – to name just a few.[1] Millions of dollars have been spent on these facilities and more will be spent operating them well into the next century.

The design, construction and management of archives buildings are changing rapidly. Our experience of what these buildings can do – and how we can best help them do it – has increased considerably over the years and, in particular, the last quarter of a century.

The Archivist

Paradoxically, while construction has proceeded on a grand scale, very little study has actually been devoted to these buildings. There have been few manuals or guidelines to assist the archivist during the design or construction process. Each institution, while often consulting with others who had built before them, basically went its own way. And there are even fewer publications dealing with the day-to-day management of an archives building.

As long ago as 1968, Robert Sharman, then with the Queensland State Archives, wrote that *'the only person who is competent to plan an archives building is one who has just completed the planning of one, and seen it erected and brought into use'.*[2]

Those words, even though they were said 30 years ago, still hold true today.

It has often been the case that the person chosen by an institution as the project officer for their new building has never previously been involved in such a project. They are not qualified architects or engineers and have little formal training in building design and construction. If they work for a government institution they are required to liaise with a Department of Works and their architects, who more than likely have never designed or built an archival facility either and often have little understanding of what such buildings are actually meant to do.

When the project is completed they return to their normal duties. Having gained a wealth of practical experience, they are generally not called upon to use it again and their knowledge is not promulgated for wider use. So, having little formal guidance to assist them at the beginning of the project, the best that could be hoped for was that they might write of their experiences at the end.

In Australia this occurred on a number of occasions. For example, in 1968 Robert Sharman wrote about his experiences with the construction of Dutton Park in Queensland;[3] Michael Saclier wrote about the Archives Office of Tasmania's new facility in 1971;[4] John Cross wrote about the construction of the Archives Office of New South Wales' Kingswood facility in 1973[5] and Vicki Warden wrote about the Queensland State Archives' new Runcorn facility in 1994.[6]

The National Archives, which has built more repositories than any other institution in this country, did not recount its collective experiences until 1994.[7]

The How To Book

What has been needed for some time is a 'How To' book which synthesises recent experiences and deals with all aspects of the building and management of archival facilities in the generic sense, not something related to one specific building. Even today, after considerable construction activity both in Australia and overseas, it is not possible to pick up a book which tells you how to design and build a records repository, and, more important, how to get it right from the very beginning.

There are some books available – by Michel Duchein, the head of the Technical Service of the Direction des Archives de France[8] and the more recent book by Christopher Kitching, the Secretary of the United Kingdom's Royal Commission on Historical Manuscripts.[9] Yet these works, particularly the first, do not account for modern technological and environmental changes which have impacted greatly on archival buildings, nor for recent changes in the appreciation of what an archives building actually is and does, so their current worth is limited. As far as Australian institutions are concerned, the books are limited even further as they are tailored to European and American markets and not Australian conditions.

There are few formal standards which will assist you either. The British issued their standard BS 5454 *Recommendations for Storage and Exhibition of Archival Documents* in 1977 and revised it in 1989.[10] In mid 1997, the International Standards Organisation released a draft standard DIS 11799:1998 *Information and Documentation – Storage Requirements for Archive and Library Materials*.[11] These two documents, while useful in their own way, could at best be described as providing only a superficial degree of guidance to the art of designing and managing an archives building.

This book, then, is an attempt to fill the void and provide a comprehensive study of the planning, construction and management of purpose-built archival repositories. It begins with an overview of what these buildings once were and how we perceive them now. It recounts experiences and lessons learned from the past and how these experiences have helped to shape our thinking today. It shows how you can design and build a repository and the essential elements of a repository and how, when these elements are fully integrated, the building should achieve the goals you have set for it.

The book contains sections on all aspects of archives buildings – including site selection, building fabric, environmental conditions, airconditioning systems, fire and security protection, as well as occupational health and safety issues. It also has a chapter on writing a design brief, working with architects and builders during the construction phase and some of the issues you are likely to encounter at this stage. As your responsibility does not end when construction is completed, it also contains a chapter on managing the facility, with reference to maintenance, pest control and disaster preparedness.

While the book is primarily intended to give prominence to Australian buildings and conditions, for which a substantial volume of experience now exists, frequent reference is made to recent developments which have occurred in other countries too.

The Lone Archivist

The USA´s National Archives and Records Administration building at College Park cost over A$250 million.
Photograph courtesy of Stewart Brothers; reproduced by kind permission of National Archives and Records Administration.

Large, modern repositories generally cost millions of dollars to build and almost as much to operate. The USA's National Archives and Records Administration facility at College Park cost over $250 million, the Queensland State Archives' facility at Runcorn cost $24 million and the National Archives' facility at East Burwood cost $9.5 million.

Yet there are archivists who work in facilities which do not cost anything remotely resembling these amounts. These are often 'lone archivists' - people who work for small companies, schools, societies or other organisations, sometimes in an honorary capacity.

Often they occupy a small part of a facility, rather than the entire building. Their needs are generally quite different to those of larger archival institutions. If they are subject to limited funding, as is often the case, they are required to develop low-cost alternatives to some of the practices described in this book.

Chapter 8 is therefore devoted to the needs of the lone archivist. It provides advice and practical solutions on issues involving archives accommodation and, while these may not always be ideal, they are probably more useful than other, more expensive options.

1   Facilities recently completed include the National Archives' building at East Burwood, Melbourne; the Queensland State Archives' building at Runcorn, south of Brisbane; BHP Pty Ltd's building at Portside, South Melbourne; the facility for the National Archives and Records Administration, USA, at College Park, Maryland (also known as Archives II); the National Archives of Canada's facility at Gatineau, near Ottawa; the Public Record Office of the United Kingdom's new building at Kew; the Public Records Office of Hong Kong's facility at Kwun Tong and the National Archives of Singapore's Canning Rise building.

2   Robert Sharman, 'New building for old. The transmigration of the Queensland State Archives', *Archives and Manuscripts*, vol. 3, no. 7, 1968, p. 35.

3   Robert Sharman, *Archives and Manuscripts*, pp. 25-35.

4   Michael Saclier, 'Buildings for archives and public records', *Proceedings of the 16th Biennial Conference of the Library Association of Australia* held in Sydney, August 1971, pp. 239-49.

5   John Cross, 'The planning and progress of the new archives building in New South Wales', *Library Association of Australia Proceedings of the 17th Biennial Conference* held in Perth, August 1973, pp. 217-34.

6   Vicki Warden, 'The New Queensland State Archives building', *Proceedings of the Australian Society of Archivists Conference* held in Townsville, 1994, pp. 48-55; Glenda I Acland also wrote briefly on this building in *Archives and Manuscripts*, vol. 21, no. 1, 1993, pp. 150-54.

7   Ted Ling, 'Silver linings: purpose built repositories - the last 25 years', *Archives and Manuscripts*, vol. 22, no. 2, 1994, pp. 360-83. In 1994 there was a brief report about the construction of the National Archives' latest facility at East Burwood in Melbourne, Victoria (Livia Iacovino, 'National Archives East Burwood repository', *Archives and Manuscripts*, vol. 22, no. 2, 1994, pp. 442-47). This article, however, was more a description of the building itself rather than an overall exposé of the design and construction process.

8   Michel Duchein, *Les Batiments d'Archives, Construction et Equipements* (published in English as *Archive Buildings and Equipment*). The French editions appeared in 1966 and 1985. The English editions were published in 1977 and 1988.

9   Christopher Kitching, *Archive Buildings in the United Kingdom 1977–1992*, London, 1993.

10 BS 5454 *Recommendations for Storage and Exhibition of Archival Documents*, London, 1977; revised 1989. This standard is currently being reviewed and a new edition is expected, probably in 1999.

11 International Standards Organisation ISO/TC46/SC10 Information and Documentation/Physical keeping of Documents DIS 11799: 1998 *Information and Documentation - Storage Requirements for Archive and Library Materials*, Copenhagen, 1998. This standard is in draft form and the final version is not expected to be released until 1999.

Chapter 1
Archives Buildings – Past and Present

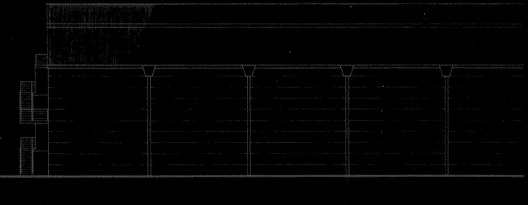

EAST E

SOUTH

Historical Overview

The earliest civilisations – Sumerian, Egyptian, Greek, Roman, Aztec and Mayan – all sought to preserve records and artefacts and used buildings, of many different kinds, to fulfil this function.

The ancient Egyptians recorded major events on papyrus and on stone. While little remains of the papyrus record, prodigious quantities of the stone (or monumental) record survive. The Egyptians' most precious objects of all were the bodies of their god kings. And, despite the fact that more than 5 000 years have elapsed, many of the bodies and the repositories which housed them survive remarkably intact. The three pyramids at Giza and the royal tombs in the Valley of the Kings are in many ways early examples of archival repositories. Archivists and the records they created were valued highly by the Egyptians. More than once, the term *Guardian of the Books* (meaning an archivist) or *Chief of the Guardians of the Books* (Head Archivist) was proudly displayed in a nobleman's tomb.

There are many other examples. Both the Greeks and Romans had archives and repositories. The Metroon in the Agora at the foot of the Acropolis was used to store the records of the Athenian Council, including their proceedings and other events. The Dead Sea scrolls survived remarkably well, wrapped and stored for 2 000 years in jars inside a cave in what is now southern Israel.

These examples demonstrate that archives, and the buildings which house them, lie at the very heart of preserving a civilisation's knowledge and culture.

Today we are no different from our predecessors. We build repositories to house and protect what we consider to be of value to us and what will be of value to future generations. We are, however, building on a legacy of what others have done before us. Our knowledge and understanding of these buildings is vastly different to what it once was and it is now an appropriate time to reflect on how we have arrived at where we are.

Solid, Safe, Secure: Building Archives Repositories in Australia

Milestones in the Origin of Modern Repositories

In the early part of this century some institutions relied on grandiose palaces, châteaux and stately buildings as the centres for their archives. In many cases the emphasis was on an impressive facade rather than a true understanding or appreciation of the real functions the buildings were supposed to perform.

The superficial impressions such buildings may give can be seen when one considers the report prepared by the historian Frederick Bladen. The Australian Government sent Bladen to observe a number of archival facilities in Europe. He duly returned and, in 1903, reported to Parliament on the 'magnificent houses and palaces' he had seen.[1] It was the magnificence of what he saw that impressed Bladen, not what the buildings themselves were actually supposed to do.

Europe and North America

The emergence of an appreciation of the way in which archives buildings function, and the need to relay this appreciation to others, probably has its origins in the catastrophic destruction caused by World War II.

In 1943, the Society of American Archivists formed a committee on archives buildings with Victor Gondos as its first chairman. Even at this early stage the Americans were looking to the post-war building period. Victor Gondos (1902-1976) was a retired naval architect. He would serve his committee for many years and would prove to be a prodigious writer on the subject of archives buildings. One of his first papers was *American Archival Architecture* published in 1947[2] and one of the last was *Archives and Record Center Buildings* published in 1970.[3] Some of his works are listed in the Select Bibliography at the end of this book.

Over the next 40 years, more committees and organisations would follow. In 1948 came the formation of the Technical Service of the Direction des Archives in France. For almost 50 years the role of this body has been to advise all levels of government in the construction and furnishing of archives buildings throughout the length and breadth of France. A brief summary of the Service's history was provided in 1990 by Danielle Neirinck, the Director of the Service.[4]

The British followed the French example in 1959. The role of the Royal Commission on Historical Manuscripts, an agency formed in the nineteenth century, was expanded to include the design and management of archives buildings. In 1993, Christopher Kitching published *Archive Buildings in the United Kingdom 1977–1992*.[5] This book gave a detailed summary of recent developments in the United Kingdom and, in addition, provided a basic overview of the many facets involved in designing and managing an archival repository.

In 1985 the International Institute for Archival Science was formed. The Institute is based in Maribor, Slovenia, and is a centre dedicated to providing information involving archives buildings and their management. To date, the Institute has assembled over 1 000 pieces of literature.[6]

And in 1988, the International Council on Archives (formed back in 1948) established its own committee on buildings and equipment.

It can be seen that what was occurring was the gradual formation of committees and government agencies whose purpose was to instruct, monitor and advise archival institutions in the design and management of their buildings. Institutions were no longer operating in isolation – at least as far as the USA and Europe were concerned – they began to have access to a range of technical expertise. However, as far as Australian archivists were concerned, such expertise was of limited value as it catered for northern hemisphere designs and conditions.

Collective literature began to appear too, rather than isolated or random journal articles. In 1956 the International Council on Archives (ICA) devoted a sizeable part of its annual journal *Archivum* to buildings.[7]

Five articles appeared in the one volume. Although all were brief, they provided valuable information. Thirty years later, the ICA would repeat this innovative idea with the 1986 issue of *Archivum* published under the banner *Modern Buildings of National Archives*.[8]

In 1964 the Society of American Archivists followed the ICA's example and dedicated an entire issue of their journal *American Archivist* to archives buildings.[9]

The year 1977 saw the emergence of the first standard, ie British Standard (BS) 5454 *Recommendations for Storage and Exhibition of Archival Documents*.[10] The standard is a brief document and naturally focuses on issues relating to buildings in the United Kingdom, but it does give some indication of the basic elements involved in repository design. A second edition appeared in 1989.

Michel Duchein.
Photograph reproduced by kind permission of International Council on Archives.

In the mid-1960s, two books were to be published in quick succession, both of which were to have a major impact on the development of archives buildings. The first was Keyes D Metcalf's *Planning Academic and Research Library Buildings* which appeared in 1965.[11] Though concerned with library buildings, it nevertheless touched on some common elements involving archival facilities, eg airconditioning, fire and security protection, shelving and floor loadings.

It would not be long before the archival profession answered the challenge issued by Metcalf. In 1966, Michel Duchein, then Director of the French Technical Service, published his great work *Les Batiments d'Archives, Construction et Equipements (Archive Buildings and Equipment)*.[12] Duchein's book was quite revolutionary. For the first time there was a single source which described in considerable detail virtually every aspect pertaining to an archival facility.

However, despite the original value of Duchein's book for Australian archivists, it was limited by virtue of its primary slant towards the European market and conditions. As a consequence of many recent and rapid changes in technology, the book is also obsolete in a number of respects. Even the second edition which appeared in 1985 (and the English version in 1988) has dated markedly.

Detours and side roads

As each milestone was passed, the number of studies proliferated and the overall knowledge base increased, some archivists seem to have made a major turn down a side road and focused on other aspects of building design. Some thought of an archives building primarily in terms of a grand statement, a monumental structure, nothing more. Others thought of these buildings solely as a source of limitless storage capacity. It seems that, on occasion, insufficient consideration was given to what it is that such buildings are intended to do.

First, the monumental structure. Reference has already been made to Frederick Bladen. But Bladen was not alone; others thought the way he did. Similar views abounded even as recently as the 1970s. Both Australia and New Zealand were visited by Dominion Archivists of Canada. Australia played host to W Kaye Lamb in 1973 and New Zealand hosted the visit of Wilfred Smith in 1978. Following these visits, reports were submitted which recommended that each country acquire a national archives building. In his report Lamb said that the Australian building:

> should be attractive in appearance, fine in quality and adequate in size: a symbol
> and visible evidence of the institution's existence and importance.[13]

Similarly, Wilfred Smith wrote in his report that:

> the visibility, location and quality of a national archives building should be a
> measure of the importance and pride that New Zealanders attach to their past
> and national identity.[14]

Nowhere in either the Lamb or the Smith reports were there any references to what it was that the buildings themselves were supposed to do, apart from being attractive or serve as a measure of importance for their owners.

Even Michel Duchein paid homage to the grand structure when he wrote:

> the use of an old building conveys little prestige on an archive service unless it is
> a stately building of character and artistic merit; this is not the case of old factories
> or warehouses, or even prisons, which are too often offered for conversion into
> archive repositories.[15]

The Australian archivist Glenda I Acland, as part of her review of the publication *The Records Continuum* in 1995, commented rather mischievously:

> I have no doubt that the most effective way of the National Archives fulfilling its
> mission statement 'To excel as an archives in the eyes of all Australians', is to have
> a purpose-built, dedicated, showy monolith in a prestige Canberra location.[16]

As with grand structures, so too there were references to archives buildings with seemingly limitless storage capacities. In 1944, the American architect Louis A Simon presented his view of a repository having what he termed a very 'special characteristic', so that:

> to the materials initially placed in it, are added documents year after year,
> generation after generation, to unpredictable limits.[17]

One has the impression that Simon regarded the typical repository as being made of rubber which would keep expanding and growing as long as the archivist needed it to. In the 1960s, when consideration was initially given to the National Archives' first true archival repository (which ultimately became Villawood), Ian Maclean, then Chief Archivist, said that the future site should 'allow for expansion for many years to come', conveying the image of a continually expanding facility.[18]

Unfortunately, some archivists allowed themselves to be seduced by the concept of size. The notion that *bigger* equates with *better* – the larger and grander the building, with its imposing facades and limitless storage capacity, the greater the organisation's status and prestige. The seduction was rendered complete with the building's location. It had to be prestigious, often with little regard paid to pollutants and proximity to potential disasters, eg lakes and rivers, or aircraft flight paths.

These views have detracted from a true appreciation of what an archives building does. Expressed in basic terms, such buildings exist to preserve records, not serve as a symbol of an organisation's corporate vanity.

Yet one person who stood apart from all of this was the American archivist Theodore Schellenberg. As long ago as 1956, he had the foresight to note:

> while the monumental features of an archival building are important, functional
> considerations are even more important. An archival building should literally be
> planned from within. Its interior should be designed for the purpose of protecting
> and making accessible to the utmost degree the contents of the building. Since an
> archival institution has the twofold objective of preserving and making available
> for use the materials in its custody, the building in which its materials are housed
> should facilitate the accomplishment of this double objective.[19]

Schellenberg puts the situation into proper perspective. There is nothing wrong with having a monumental building or an imposing facade, provided it is secondary to the building's *raison d'être* of preserving records. If kept in its subservient role, one can have both. It is when the desire to have a monumental structure assumes greater prominence that the essential reasons for the building's creation will start to falter.

Milestones in Australia

It will not have passed unnoticed that all the milestones referred to previously have occurred in Europe or North America. But there have also been a number of milestones in Australia. They have not involved the formation of government advisory bodies or committees. There were none. In fact, none exist even today. They did not take the form of major publications or standards, though there are some of these. Rather, the milestones in Australia have taken the form of actual construction. For Australia's size and population, there has been considerable activity and a wealth of knowledge has been gained.

For the Archives Office of Tasmania's Berriedale facility, an existing building was refurbished.
Photograph reproduced by kind permission of Archives Office of Tasmania.

At the national level, in 1965 the National Archives took its first initiative towards the selection of a site and new facility in the western suburbs of Sydney. A site at Villawood was finally procured in 1969 and the construction of two buildings commenced shortly after. The first building – a non-airconditioned facility designed primarily for temporary value records – was completed in 1972. The second building, a multi-storey, fully airconditioned complex, was completed in August 1975. The Archives has since built repositories in all capital cities. The national network was finally completed with the opening of East Burwood in Melbourne, Victoria, in February 1994.

At the State level, in 1961 the Archives Office of New South Wales began to plan for the acquisition of a site and the construction of a purpose-built repository also west of Sydney. A site at Kingswood was soon acquired, though ultimately would be surrendered in favour of another. Financial constraints, however, would delay the commencement of construction until 1973 and the building would not be completed until 1975. The Archives Office has expanded Kingswood on a number of occasions since that time.

The Queensland State Archives built its first facility at Dutton Park, which was opened in July 1968. It is open to debate, but this was perhaps the first true archival facility in Australia. The facility was not a requisitioned warehouse; it was designed and built with the express purpose of storing permanent value records. Ultimately, Dutton Park would be abandoned in favour of a new facility at Runcorn, south of Brisbane; the building was opened in 1993. This new facility is currently undergoing an expansion.

The Archives Office of Tasmania completed a 10-storey library and archival facility in Murray Street, Hobart, in 1971. An existing facility at Berriedale was acquired, refurbished and completed in 1985.

BHP Pty Ltd completed their purpose-built repository at Portside in 1995.
Photograph courtesy of Salta Properties; reproduced by kind permission of BHP Archives.

And, finally, in 1998, the Public Record Office of Victoria is scheduled to commence the construction of its first purpose-built facility on a site only 4 kilometres from Melbourne's central business district.

A number of companies have acquired repositories, though these have mostly consisted of refurbished warehouses. One major exception is one of Australia's largest companies, the mining and steel producing company BHP Pty Ltd, which completed a purpose-built facility at Portside, South Melbourne, in May 1995.

A few general points can be made about the facilities referred to above. First, by today's standards Dutton Park and Murray Street, Hobart, would be hard pressed to qualify as dedicated archival facilities. Yet they were purpose-built for their time and, more important, were not attempts at the grand statement. They were functional first and monumental second.

Second, the Villawood and Kingswood facilities were, and still are, the largest facilities built in Australia. All facilities built since have been considerably smaller. It is indeed ironic that the country's largest archives buildings were built at roughly the same time and are located only a few kilometres apart.

So now, after more than 50 years of frenetic activity worldwide and almost 30 years in Australia, the milestones have had a cumulative effect. They have added to our overall sum of knowledge and have brought us to a position where we can more appropriately understand and appreciate the value of an archival repository, what functions it performs and precisely how it operates.

In the past 12 months, the National Archives of Australia has had a unique opportunity to apply the experience of the past and build on the many lessons learned. The Archives has for many years been seeking a national headquarters building prominently located in the national capital. Early in 1997, an opportunity presented itself to occupy one of the original buildings constructed to enable Canberra to fulfil its role as the capital of Australia. While the building was in an excellent location with a good architectural presentation, it required major refurbishment and fitout. A sum of approximately $10 million dollars was allocated to the task which was commenced mid-1997. The building became fully functional in April 1998.

The building, known as the National Archives, accommodates full facilities for research including a holding repository. In addition, it houses galleries enabling the exhibition of selected archival holdings. Staff facilities to support these functions and provide for the national administration for the organisation are also included. Design has focused on producing a building which externally projects an archival identity and internally provides an environment which is both friendly to users and the records.

Kingswood, Archives Office of New South Wales, is one of the two largest facilities built in Australia.
Photograph reproduced by kind permission of Archives Office of New South Wales.

Archival repositories of the 1960s and 1990s

Once they were great stone or concrete structures that were meant to be impressive. They were meant to reflect the grandeur and status of their owners. Once they were supposed to provide limitless storage capacity. In the Cold War period, they were even meant to be nuclear bomb proof. And if the institution was fortunate, sometimes the building might also protect the records stored within it. It seemed, however, that this feature was in some cases almost an afterthought.

In the 1960s, a prime factor in the design and location of the purpose-built repository was its resistance to nuclear explosions. Both the Villawood and Kingswood repositories are large, almost monolithic structures and resistance to nuclear explosion certainly played a part in the early stages of their design.

Since the 1970s, however, a number of changes have taken place. First, repositories are generally becoming smaller (College Park in the USA being the notable exception to this rule) and storage areas are far more compartmentalised than was previously the case. This change has not occurred solely as a response to stringent economic conditions. It dovetails with the recognition that facilities are no longer monoliths existing simply to provide limitless records storage. There is now a much greater understanding of a building's total structural integrity. Archivists now think in terms of a building's capability of *sustaining* environmental conditions, not just *creating* them. They think of the entire building structure – eg walls, roofs and floor – as a means of aiding this process. Repositories are now designed and built with the intention of providing a 'total preservation environment for the storage of archives',[20] a point which will be discussed in more detail in chapter 2. For this reason, repositories with smaller storage spaces are much more likely to meet this requirement than larger, open plan buildings.

Second, having smaller storage spaces makes it easier to contain a fire should one ever occur. A fire in a large, open-plan floor area is extremely difficult to contain, even with a sprinkler system.

Third, there is a much greater awareness of what airconditioning systems can and cannot do. With a fervour bordering on fanaticism, many archivists argued the need for airconditioning systems in their purpose-built facilities. Such a practice was based on the mistaken belief that if a comprehensive system was installed all would be well. Whatever other failings the building might have, airconditioning systems would overcome them. It is now known and understood that this view is entirely erroneous. In essence, the building's fabric must create a sealed environment that is then complemented by an airconditioning system. The system by itself cannot make up for deficiencies in design and construction.

Fourth, technology has had a major impact, one example being the advent of sophisticated building management systems. These systems can operate most of the building's airconditioning plant, lighting, fire and security systems. They can also monitor environmental conditions and make the necessary adjustments to the plant whenever conditions are outside nominated parameters.

Fifth, there is greater recognition given to environmental concerns and to the development of 'green' buildings. To give just one example, in the past many buildings had halon gas as part of their fire fighting systems. Halon has been shown to be detrimental to the ozone layer and, as a result, has had to be removed.

Last, the comfort and safety of staff and visitors within and around the building are given far more emphasis than they once were.

How do we define an archival repository today?

So, what then is an archival repository, one designed and built in the 1990s?

The 1989 edition of British Standard (BS) 5454 defines a repository as:

> a place of storage for documents, so constructed and maintained as to prevent damage, decay and unauthorised access, and to furnish, for archival documents, proper conditions of custody.[21]

In the second English edition (1988) of his book *Archive Buildings and Equipment*, Michel Duchein uses a more elaborate definition. He insists that the repository needs to meet four fundamental requirements:

- the preservation of documents in complete safety, which requires sound premises, protected against fire, humidity, excessive sunlight, insects, rodents, thieves, etc;
- the production of documents to users, which requires space for listing, packing and labelling, as well as catalogues and inventories, reading rooms, reception and public information areas;
- repair of damaged documents; and
- reproduction of documents: microfilm, photocopies, etc.[22]

The National Archives uses the term *purpose-built repository*, the crucial part of the term being *purpose-built*. A repository is not simply a building in which to store records. Any building can perform this function. Even a tin shed, garage, attic, basement, or a box under the bed, will provide some protection, albeit highly unsatisfactory.

In essence, the purpose-built repository of the 1990s is designed and constructed to perform three principal functions:

- it must protect records stored within it from atmospheric pollution, fire, flooding, pest infestation and vandalism;
- it must provide facilities for clients to consult the records being held within; and
- it must provide a safe and comfortable environment for staff and visitors.

The first two functions are a reflection of the views espoused by Theodore Schellenberg in 1956. They are as valid now as they were then. The third criterion reflects the emphasis given to occupational health and safety, a trend which emerged in the 1980s and continues to the present day.

The major lesson that has been learned over the past 50 years is that repositories are not just buildings made of concrete, bricks and steel, with an airconditioning system thrown in for good measure. These features working in isolation will achieve nothing. Repositories are functional entities; it is the integration of these features that make the building work.

1   F M Bladen, 'Report on European archives', *Parliamentary Papers*, vol. II, 1903, pp. 993–997.

2   Victor Gondos, 'American archival architecture', *Bulletin of the American Institute of Architects*, vol. 1, no. 4, 1947, pp. 27–32.

3   Victor Gondos, *Archives and Record Center Buildings*, Washington, 1970.

4   Danielle Neirinck, 'The role of the Technical Service of the Direction des Archives in the construction of archival buildings in France', *American Archivist*, vol. 53, no. 1, 1990, pp. 140–146.

5   Christopher Kitching, *Archive Buildings in the United Kingdom 1977–1992*, London, 1993.

6   The Institute has a site on the Internet (www.pokarh-mb.si/miaz.html) which is well worth visiting.

7   *Archivum*, vol. VI, 1956, section II, 'Batiments d'archives' (Archival Buildings).

8   *Archivum*, vol. XXXI, 1986.

9   *American Archivist*, vol. 27, no. 4, 1964, pp. 467–502.

10 British Standard (BS) 5454, *Recommendations for Storage and Exhibition of Archival Documents*, London, 1977; revised 1989. As a postscript, in 1989 the United Kingdom Public Record Office, Royal Commission on Historical Manuscripts and the Scottish Record Office jointly issued *A Standard for Record Repositories* which includes an appendix Guidelines for record repositories modelled on the British Standard (see Brian S Smith, 'A standard for record repositories', *Journal of the Society of Archivists*, vol. 12, no. 2, 1991, pp. 114-122). A second edition of this standard, albeit with minor variations, was issued in 1997.

11 Keyes D Metcalf, *Planning Academic and Research Library Buildings*, New York, 1965.

12 Michel Duchein, *Archive Buildings and Equipment*, Munich, 1988.

13 W Kaye Lamb, 'Development of a National Archives', *Parliamentary Paper* no. 16 of 1973, pp. 8–9.

14 Wilfred Smith, *Archives in New Zealand*, Archives and Records Association of New Zealand, Wellington, 1978, p. 21.

15 Michel Duchein, *Archive Buildings and Equipment*, p. 21. This reference appeared in the first edition (1977). In the second edition (1988) it was deleted.

16 Glenda I Acland, 'Review of *The Records Continuum*', *Archives and Manuscripts*, vol. 23, no. 1, 1995, p. 102.

17 Louis A Simon, 'Some observations on planning archives buildings', Bulletin of the National Archives (USA) *Buildings and Equipment for Archives*, No. 6, 1944, p. 4.

18 NAA: Commonwealth Archives Office; A750, General correspondence files, annual single number series, item 1964/147, f. 11.

19 T R Schellenberg, 'Modern archival buildings', *Archivum*, vol. VI, 1956, p.89.

20 Vicki Warden, verbal quote to the author, August 1994.

21 British Standard (BS) 5454, p. 2.

22 Michel Duchein, *Archive Buildings and Equipment*, p. 26.

Chapter 2
The Site and the Building

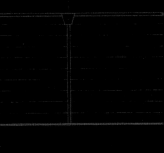

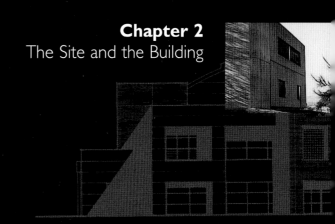

EAST EL

SOUTH E

The Site

Having discussed what an archival building actually is and does, we can now consider how to actually create this.

The first step in the process of creating an archival building is the selection of a site. Site selection is vital in ensuring that each building will ultimately perform to its maximum potential and your institution can provide an appropriate service to your clients.

Selecting the ideal site

In 1956, the German archivist Georg Winter listed five key factors which should apply when selecting the site for an archival repository.[1]
The factors were as follows:

- nearness to agencies;
- nearness to cultural and research institutions;
- nearness to the centre of public life;
- away from fire-threatening establishments and from districts subject to dampness, flooding or harmful airborne gas and dust particles; and
- away from closely built and densely populated areas.

These factors have been dutifully copied and commented upon by a number of archivists, including Victor Gondos in 1964,[2] Robert Sharman in 1968[3] and Michael Saclier in 1971.[4]

The first two of Winter's criteria relate to the clients with whom the institution would be dealing. However, given that most agencies, cultural and research centres are based in or near cities, proximity would not be practical with today's high real estate costs.

With respect to the third criterion – proximity to the centre of public life – the size of land that a repository consumes, the general scarcity of land near such centres, and its prohibitive costs even when it is available, now render this impractical.

Winter's fourth criterion – clearance from fire threatening establishments (eg oil refineries, chemical plants) and areas subject to dampness, flood or airborne contaminants – is by today's standards the most significant.

The last criterion – separation from closely built and densely populated areas – can, in some cases, refer to the same areas where agencies congregate and cultural centres are also located. It would seem that some of Winter's selection criteria were mutually exclusive.

In order to identify and evaluate factors pertaining to site selection today it is worthwhile to look briefly at how the National Archives chose the sites for its Villawood and East Burwood repositories. Villawood was acquired in the 1960s and was the Archives' first truly purpose-built repository. It remains the largest archival facility operated by the National Archives and for many years was the largest in Australia, being relegated to second place only recently by the Archives Office of New South Wales' Kingswood facility.

East Burwood, though considerably smaller than Villawood, represents the National Archives' most recent site selection.

The National Archives of Australia's Villawood site met all the selection criteria in 1969.

The selection of Villawood had its origins in 1965. The Archives (then known as the Commonwealth Archives Office) occupied a site at Maroubra, south of Sydney. The land was owned by the Commonwealth Government but was ultimately to be returned to the New South Wales State Government. There were strong indications that by 1970 the site would no longer be available to the Archives.

Almost from the outset, the evidence shows that the Archives chose to build anew rather than refurbish an existing facility, though for a brief moment it did consider purchasing such a building at Rushcutters Bay, a site close to Sydney's centre.

The Archives specified a number of factors that would render an intended site suitable.[5] These factors were:

- sufficient size, 4-5 acres would be required;
- free of dust and industrial smoke;
- no more than 10 miles from the city, with good access by road and, preferably, public transport; and
- adjacent to another Commonwealth facility so that the two might share common security measures.

Over the next four years, sites to the north-west, south and west of Sydney were all considered. Such sites included Rydalmere, Botany, Bass Hill, Zetland, Pyrmont, Padstow, Ryde and Lane Cove. All were rejected as being too small, or too close to pollutants or other dangers.

Even land near the Navy's Armaments Depot at Rydalmere was considered and fortunately rejected. Curiously, the principal reason given for the rejection of the site was the fact that it was 'too far from the city to economically and efficiently provide a service to Commonwealth Departments'.[6] The risk of possible explosion was only listed second.

By May 1969, five sites were under active consideration and for the first time Commonwealth land at Villawood appeared among the list of contenders. The other sites were Randwick, Rydalmere (not the previously rejected Armaments Depot site), Bankstown and St Marys.

Villawood is about 25 kilometres south-west of Sydney. The site was agreed by all concerned to be the most suitable. It was Commonwealth land, owned by the Departments of Immigration and Army. It was 4.5 acres, though with some negotiation with the other departments this could be increased to a more appropriate 6 acres. It was adjacent to another Commonwealth facility (a migrant hostel) and was only 40–50 minutes drive from the city. Ironically, Villawood is considerably further from the city than the Rydalmere site which was rejected because of the distance factor.

The land was sloping, but this did not appear to present any problems. It was also possible that in the future, additional land could be acquired from the nearby migrant hostel allowing for further development. Last, the purpose for which the site was to be used was considered unlikely to draw any objection from the local Council.

There was, however, one negative factor. Vacant land on the southern side of the site was owned by a paint company. It was felt that the Council would not allow the company to undertake any 'obnoxious activities on the site' and it was noted that the company already had a factory operating elsewhere.[7] So any environmental concerns appear to have been allayed.

Ownership of the Villawood site was transferred to the Archives in September 1969.

Nowhere in the early documentation were there any references to the possibility of flooding. However, in January 1970 (four months after the site was acquired), at an interdepartmental committee meeting for the new building, it was noted, perhaps rather fortuitously, that creek flood levels did not present a problem.[8]

The Villawood site is quite small by comparison with those used by other organisations, but it has, for the most part, worked well for the Archives. It has allowed for the early construction of two large buildings which, even today, more than adequately meet the organisation's needs.

Yet there was, and still is, a drawback to the Villawood site. The early correspondence made no reference to several factories located within the Villawood area, only a short distance from the Archives' site. It is probable that the significance of these factories was never fully appreciated at the time. If the filtration systems of these factories are inadequate, then their waste by-products can, if wind conditions are favourable, be caught in the Archives' own airconditioning system, contaminating its filters.

Case Study Number 2 – *Selection of National Archives' East Burwood Site*

The National Archives' most recent repository is at East Burwood, Melbourne

Now compare the selection criteria for Villawood with the criteria used for the site chosen for the Archives' most recent repository in Melbourne, Victoria.[9] As before, the Archives was seeking to replace an existing facility (in this case a former dry cleaning factory at Brighton) with a purpose-built repository.

The selection criteria were as follows:
- clear from all heavy industry (chemical plants, rubber factories, hospital waste);
- elevated to avoid possibility of flooding from creeks, rivers or stormwater drains; and
- close proximity to a major freeway connecting the site with the Melbourne central business district and within a reasonable distance of a mode of public transport.

After examining a number of possibilities, East Burwood was chosen. The land was the right size for the Archives' needs (1.2 hectares). It was owned by the Australian Broadcasting Corporation. It was surrounded by houses and a technology park. It was elevated so there should be no possibility of flooding. Last, it was only 22 kilometres from Melbourne and was relatively close to a highway and to public transport (a tram line). The land had previously been used as part of the Tally Ho Boys Home and, at the time of its purchase by the Archives, had been cleared and the only occupants were grazing horses.

The East Burwood site was acquired in 1992 at a cost slightly below $1.5 million. On this occasion, the Archives was required to purchase the site rather than simply have ownership transferred from another Commonwealth agency as was the case with Villawood.

Almost 25 years had elapsed between the selection of the Villawood and East Burwood sites yet it can be seen that site selection criteria had remained very similar.

Site selection today – external factors

When selecting the site for a purpose-built repository many factors will come into play. No matter how large or how small the site is, and regardless of what kind of records are to be held in the facility, each site needs to be assessed against a number of criteria. Furthermore, it is not just the site itself, but the surrounds of each site that also need to be considered. These criteria apply regardless of whether your building will be new or refurbished.

At the outset it can generally be assumed that it will not be possible to choose a site in or near the city centre. Even if land is available, its prohibitive costs will render this option impractical, hence sites outside of the city will more than likely have to be considered.

1. Well clear of pollutants – factories, chemical plants, munitions factories.

The site should be clear of all forms of heavy industry, eg oil refineries, chemical plants, paint or rubber factories. In short, any type of factory or plant that is capable of emitting pollutants. A light industrial area is preferable, such as a warehousing estate or a technology park. Even as far back as 1966 when the National Archives was assessing sites for its first facility in Sydney a 'light industrial area' was considered the ideal location.[10]

2. Well clear of tracts of water.

The site must be well clear of the ocean, rivers, creeks and dams. In short, any major water supply. The reason for this is twofold. The first – and more obvious – is to guard against the possibility of flooding or seepage. The second is that proximity to the ocean can

The construction of the National Archives of Australia's Mitchell facility shows the built-up nature of the site, to guard against possible flooding.
Photographs by Jutta Hosel; reproduced by kind permission of the National Archives of Australia.

cause salt corrosion to the building's structure. It should be remembered that flood possibilities may not be immediately apparent. It will benefit you to make a study of the site and its surrounds and ascertain if the area has been prone to flooding in the past.

The National Archives' facility in the north Canberra suburb of Mitchell is located on a 100-year flood plain, hence the site has been elevated to guard against the possibility of flooding.

SITE SELECTION CRITERIA

Well clear of pollutants - factories, chemical plants

Well clear of tracts of water

Well clear of a major airport and not directly below a flight path

Close to a highway or freeway connecting the site to the city
or where most clients are located

TABLE 1 SITES CHOSEN BY MAJOR ARCHIVAL INSTITUTIONS

Facility	Institution	Distance from the CBD	Site Surrounds
Villawood	National Archives	25 kms from Sydney	Migrant hostel, migrant detention centre, paint factory, houses
East Burwood	National Archives	22 kms from Melbourne	Houses, technology park
Kingswood	Archives Office of New South Wales	55 kms from Sydney	Houses, University of Western Sydney
Runcorn	Queensland State Archives	19 kms from Brisbane	Houses, bushland
Berriedale	Archives Office of Tasmania	12 kms from Hobart	Highway, factory, houses
Portside	BHP Pty Ltd	6 kms from Melbourne	Business park
Wellington	National Archives of New Zealand	0 kms from Wellington	Cultural buildings, government offices
Nouville	Archives Territoriales, New Caldeonia	3 kms from Noumea	Forest
College Park	National Archives and Records Administration, USA	16 kms from Washington	Houses, forest
Gatineau	National Archives of Canada	12 kms from Ottawa	Fields, rainwater run-off pond
Kew	Public Record Office, UK	16 kms from London	Houses
Koblenz	Bundesarchiv, Germany	80 kms from Bonn	Houses
Arningedepan	Riksarkivet, Sweden	15 kms from Stockholm	Light industry, small factories
Ulleval Hageby	Riksarkivet, National Archives of Norway	8 kms from Oslo	Forest, houses
Beijing	Beijing Municipal Archives	9 kms from Beijing	Houses
Shanghai	Shanghai Municipal Archives	10 kms from Shanghai	Commercial buildings and colleges
Kwun Tong	Public Records Office, Hong Kong	20 kms from Hong Kong	Government housing estate, church
Taejon	Government Archives and Records Service, Republic of Korea	155 kms from Seoul	Apartments and offices
Canning Rise	National Archives of Singapore	0 kms from Singapore	Cultural institutions

3. Well clear of a major airport and not directly below an aircraft flight path.

The site should be clear of major airports and not directly below a flight path. Otherwise there is the risk of an aircraft crashing into the facility, or losing a wheel and having it fall through the roof. Second, there is the ever present problem of pollution that aircraft exhaust can generate.

4. Close to a freeway/transport connecting the site to the city or where the bulk of clients are located.

Last, the site should be close to public transport and a freeway/highway to the city. It should not actually be on the freeway – a few blocks behind is preferable. This way there is the advantage of rapid access to clients and the avoidance of vehicular pollution.

To a certain extent the site selection criteria listed above are subjective. Just how near or far should the site be from a factory, flood plain, or the city centre? Each institution will need to make its own judgement.

As far as distance from the city centre is concerned, less than 1 hour's drive on a freeway would seem reasonable. The distance and time taken to reach the centre can be countered by cheaper land costs and the reduced air pollution that will be obtained by moving away from the city.

Most of the above criteria are self evident, yet there are other criteria which might easily be overlooked. As you would when buying your own home, you should look very closely at who will be the neighbours for your new building.

Pollutants could include a suburban garage with underground fuel tanks and the risk of an explosion. This is currently the case with the National Archives' Darwin facility.

Undesirable neighbours might not necessarily include chemical plants or paint factories. They might include a jail – the Queensland State Archives was for many years based at Dutton Park, near the Boggo Road jail. The National Archives' Villawood facility is adjacent to the Villawood Migrant Detention Centre. More than once, persons attempting to avoid deportation have used the Archives' site to aid their escape. Last, undesirable neighbours could even refer to a nearby hotel where drunks might congregate and subject the facility to vandalism.

It should also never be assumed that choosing a site near a city will render your institution safe from natural disasters. There are many such disasters which have occurred either near to, or even within, a city, eg the Brisbane floods of 1974, the effects of Cyclone Tracy on Darwin in 1974, the Ash Wednesday fires of 1983, the Newcastle earthquake of 1989 and the Townsville and Katherine floods of 1998. And in recent years there have been major industrial fires in locations such as Alexandria (Sydney) and Coode Island (Melbourne). (See chapter 6 for ways of dealing with the aftermath of disasters.)

The table on page 26 provides an indication where other institutions have located their buildings and who their neighbours were.

Internal factors – the site itself

Now to the site itself. As there were external factors to be considered, so too there are internal factors. There are a number of questions that you will need to ask about the site, most of which are quite basic, but in some cases to obtain relevant information detailed research will be required. For example:

How big is the site and will it allow for future expansion?

Is the land level and, if not, will sloping land cause major construction problems?

Are there any facilities on the site already and, if so, will they be costly to remove?

What was the land used for previously? Are there any contaminants on the site? Even if it is a clear site now it may once have been used as a dump for industrial waste, or even as a sheep dipping site.

Is there any indication of pest infestations, particularly termites? A pest report should be sought.

You should also commission an assessment of the soil to ensure the bedrock will allow for firm foundations, and to further ensure that there is no clay (which has undesirable expansive qualities) or an over supply of rocks or boulders that will require costly removal.

If due consideration and adequate weighting are given to the external and internal criteria, as outlined above, you will not only avoid some of the mistakes that have been made in the past, but you will ensure that your archives has a site that will enable the construction, or refurbishment, of a facility that should meet all the demands placed upon it.

A word of warning

However much you may wish to choose the ideal site for your institution, it should be recognised that in many instances political factors may come into play – at both the government or business level. You may well be compelled to accept a site that is less than ideal. The government or business may have surplus land which you do not consider will meet your requirements yet this may be the only site offered.

There have been numerous instances of organisations having to locate their facility many miles from the central business district, on flood plains or below aircraft flight paths because this was the only site they were permitted to accept. If the decision is made to go to such a site, you can argue the case but then must be prepared to accept the inevitable and attempt to minimise the effects of such a decision.

TABLE 2 RECENT SITE SIZES AND BUILDING STORAGE CAPACITIES

Facility	Institution	Site Area (in hectares)	Storage Capacity (in kilometres)
Villawood	National Archives	2.5	195
East Burwood	National Archives	1.2	50
Kingswood	Archives Office of New South Wales	22.26	196
Runcorn	Queensland State Archives	8	40
Berriedale	Archives Office of Tasmania	0.4	16.5
Portside	BHP Pty Ltd	0.6	150
Wellington	National Archives of New Zealand	0.55	80
Nouville	Archives Territoriales, New Caldeonia	1	6.5
College Park	National Archives and Records Administration, USA	13.4	837
Gatineau	National Archives of Canada	23.7	165
Kew	Public Record Office, UK [*]	4.93	74
Koblenz	Bundesarchiv, Germany	3.46	112
Arningedepan	Riksarkivet, Sweden	0.6	80 (plus an additional 80)
Ulleval Hageby	Riksarkivet, National Archives of Norway	2.08	85 (plus an additional 36)
Beijing	Beijing Municipal Archives	1	20
Shanghai	Shanghai Municipal Archives	0.22	21
Kwun Tong	Public Records Office, Hong Kong	0.07	11
Taejon	Government Archives and Records Service, Republic of Korea	0.85	25.6
Canning Rise	National Archives of Singapore	0.6	16

How much land is sufficient?

This question was raised earlier, yet in reality it has no answer. Each institution needs to assess the issue based on its own needs. However, the following table outlines the size of some relevant sites and the storage capacities of the facilities built on them.

Expressed solely in terms of records storage, a rule of thumb is that the land should be of such a size that will permit the construction of a facility to house your initial holdings as well as intake over the next eight to ten years. In addition, it should enable a second facility – whether it be another building, an extension to the first building, or simply another storey – which will accommodate growth for another 10 to 20 years. In essence, the site should enable you to function for the next 25 to 30 years.

For example, the National Archives' East Burwood site is 1.2 hectares. The present building consists of two storeys and a mezzanine level and has a total storage capacity of 50 kilometres. In addition, there is accommodation for staff and public researchers. The site is sufficient to allow the expansion of the building in either of two separate directions.

Buy or lease?

One question that has not been considered before now is the issue of whether you should purchase the site and building outright or whether you should have a developer undertake the purchase on your behalf and then lease the facility back from the developer over a given period of time, say 20 years.

In the 1980s, the National Archives and State Records, South Australia, jointly developed a new facility at Gepps Cross, 10 kilometres north of Adelaide, South Australia. The two organisations prepared a design brief and the facility was built by a developer in exchange for a 12-year lease. The facility was completed in 1987 and the lease expires in 1999. Each organisation occupies approximately half of the building. The facility provides over 69 kilometres of storage capacity. The office areas are airconditioned but the main storage areas are not.

Additionally, BHP Pty Ltd's Portside facility was built by a developer in exchange for a 10-year lease. The facility can provide up to 150 kilometres of storage.

As with so many other aspects involving repository management, the leasing option contains both advantages and disadvantages. Leasing is attractive in that it provides initial low costs, the bulk of the early expenses being borne by the developer. Second, if you are a private company you may be able to achieve tax concessions on your leasing payments.

There are disadvantages, however. You are locked into a fixed, long-term arrangement. Overall costs will be higher throughout the length of the lease. Last, very careful consideration needs to be given to your building's specifications. Otherwise there will be scope for the developer to cut corners with the result that he will pocket any savings as you still have to pay the agreed lease costs, even if there are savings made during construction.

Refurbishing an existing building or constructing a new one

Modern literature, particularly European, has contained cogent reasons for the acquisition of existing buildings and converting them to serve as repositories. Reference is made not only to the use of warehouses, but to the possible use of castles, châteaux and monasteries. Given the age of these latter buildings, and their ability to maintain stable environmental conditions, their use as archival facilities would seem to be quite valid.[11]

The National Archives of New Zealand chose to house its archives in a former printing works in the heart of Wellington. New Zealand, however, represents 1 of the few instances where a national archival institution has pursued the refurbishment option in recent times.

The National Archives of New Zealand is housed in a former printing works in the heart of Wellington.
Photograph reproduced by kind permission of the National Archives of New Zealand.

Refurbishment has never really presented as a viable option in Australia given the paucity of suitable buildings and a recognition that, for the most part, older buildings cannot match the conditions afforded by a new facility designed and built for the purpose of records preservation. Even former warehouses or similar facilities are unlikely to present themselves as suitable candidates. It is not an easy task to find a building which has – or could have even after a costly refurbishment – a sound structure, with appropriate floor loadings, suitable airconditioning and which is located in an ideal site.

When the National Archives was considering sites for its first building in Sydney, the search was confined to locations which would permit the construction of a new facility. There was, however, 1 exception. In 1967, a building near the city centre at Rushcutters Bay was actively promoted to the point where an urgent Cabinet submission was contemplated to enable purchase of the site. The Archives was attracted to the building due to its size and proximity to the city. The proposal lapsed only because the Department of Works advised that the cost of refurbishment, including strengthening upper floor loadings to allow for the installation of mobile shelving, and the installation of airconditioning and sprinklers, made the proposal uneconomic.[12]

A similar situation arose for East Burwood. Brief consideration was given to a former facility owned by a photographic company. The site was rejected because it failed to meet the Archives' site selection criteria. Likewise, when considering their new facilities, the Queensland State Archives and BHP Pty Ltd were unable to find existing buildings which would meet their parameters, even after refurbishment.

However, the Archives Office of Tasmania did purchase and refurbish an existing facility. The building was a former bulk steel store, located at Berriedale, north of Hobart, and was purchased by the Archives in 1985. It was chosen as it provided the space the Archives needed and the floor loadings were adequate. The acquisition of an existing facility was not, however, the Archives' preferred choice. It had originally decided to build a new facility but in the end government cost cutting, and the urgent need for a facility, necessitated the purchase of an existing building.

The National Archives of Singapore has adopted a dual approach for its new facility at Canning Rise. There are two buildings. The first, which contains the office and conservation areas, is a former school building which has been refurbished. The adjacent second building, which is used for records storage, is new.

It is noteworthy that the established Australian trend to build new facilities is now being seen in other countries. Recent buildings in North America, Europe and Asia are all new, not refurbished.

As with a new building, an existing facility must obviously accommodate your needs now and well into the future and careful planning is needed to ensure that it does. Apart from the initial attraction of ready availability and cheaper costs, there are many problems that may be enountered by attempting to refurbish an existing building.

First, take a good look at the building's external structure. Are there signs of ageing – cracking, rising damp or other problems? What are the extent of these problems and how costly will they be to repair?

Next, consider the building's fabric – walls, floor and roof. Is it sufficiently integrated to help maintain stable environmental conditions? Will the walls and floors of the proposed storage areas prohibit moisture penetration? If not, what is the likely cost of overcoming these deficiencies?

Now the roof and the drainage system. Is the roof pitched and in good condition? A flat roof is more likely to allow rainwater into the building. Does the drainage system have sufficient capacity to enable rapid removal of rainwater even in a severe storm?

If the facility has wooden floors, there are a number of issues to be addressed. First, it may not be possible to effectively seal them in order to maintain stable conditions. Second, will they take the weight of mobile shelving? Third, have they been treated to ensure they are fire resistant?

At Canning Rise, the National Archives of Singapore used a former school building for an office and conservation area (top) whilst an adjacent new building (above) is for records storage.
Photographs by Ted Ling.

Even if they have, wooden floors are far more likely to burn than concrete or steel floors.

There may be a preponderance of pillars in the storage areas which will restrict the placement of mobile shelving.

The building may lack airconditioning and the cost of installing a system will be substantial. If there is an airconditioning system available, its current operating state will need to be assessed and a number of questions will need to be asked. What kind of refrigerant does the system use? For example, older systems may contain chlorofluorocarbons (CFCs) which are now prohibited in accordance with the Montreal Protocol of 1987.[13] An assessment will also need to be made of the airconditioning ducts and whether they will require cleaning. Likewise, the building's electrical and plumbing systems will need to be scrutinised and replaced or repaired if found to be defective.

Older buildings may have inadequate or non-existent fire or security protection. They are less likely to meet current safety standards. The walls and doors of the storage areas may not have adequate fire ratings. Fire exits and fire escapes (stairways) may need to be installed at an added cost.

You should pay particular attention to the building's floor loadings and ascertain if they will be suitable to accommodate mobile shelving. This is a very basic question given the extraordinary weights that will be carried, eg a double-sided mobile five bays wide will, when fully laden, weigh in excess of 3 tonnes.

If an existing building is being used, mobile shelving will more than likely need to operate on raised tracks, rather than tracks laid below the floor. Thus, false floors or ramps will be needed to allow the movement of trolleys in and out of each aisle and to prevent staff tripping over the tracks. The installation of false floors or ramps will represent another cost.

Are there windows in the storage areas? They will need to be covered.

Older buildings may have some of the environmental problems that newer buildings will not. For example, asbestos was commonly used in wall insulation and as lagging around water pipes, even as recently as the 1970s. It is highly dangerous to allow it to remain, particularly if it is loose, and it is very costly to have removed. Both the Archives Office of Tasmania's Berriedale facility and the National Archives of New Zealand's facility in Wellington had asbestos which had to be removed.

Light fittings in older buildings may contain polychlorinated biphenyls (PCBs) – a chemical used in the capacitors of fluorescent lighting until the mid 1970s. Again, to allow it to remain is dangerous, yet to have it removed is very costly.

An older building may have pest problems, such as termites, and a very thorough pest inspection should be sought.

If your institution is seriously considering refurbishing an existing building, all of the above factors need to be taken into account. Otherwise, what begins as a cheaper alternative may, in the long run, be more costly and, in any event, not be able to provide the conditions you are actually seeking to achieve.

REFURBISHING AN EXISTING BUILDING – SOME FACTORS TO CONSIDER

Building exterior	what condition is it in; signs of movement, cracking, rising damp?
Walls/floors	are they sufficient to prevent moisture penetration; is there any sign of rising damp?
Walls/doors	are they fire rated; for how long?
Roof	is it pitched to ensure rapid rainwater run off? what condition is it in; rusting, leaking?
Drainage	what condition is it in; rusting, leaking; will it enable the prompt removal of rainwater in a severe storm?
Floors	are they wooden; are the loadings sufficient to allow for mobile shelving?
Airconditioning system	what condition is it in; can it provide the environmental conditions needed; what refrigerants does it use?
Ductwork	does it require cleaning?
Fire protection	what is available and does it meet current standards and requirements?
Security protection	what is available and does it meet current standards and requirements?
Electrical system	what condition is it in; will it require an overhaul or complete replacement?
Plumbing system	what condition is it in; will it require an overhaul or complete replacement?
Asbestos	is it present and, if so, is it loose or secured?
Light fittings	are polychlorinated biphenyls (PCBs) present?
Pests	is there any evidence of pest infestation?

Locating the building on the site

Each site and each building are unique, which makes it difficult to set precise requirements, but there are a number of observations that can be made concerning the placement of a new building on its site.

Before siting the building on the final plan, you should be aware of where all the main services in the area are located. The precise location of all power lines, water supply, stormwater drains and sewer lines should be ascertained. If the building is to be set well back on a large site, the connections to these services will be made more expensive than might otherwise be the case.

When siting the building, you should also take into account the effects of solar radiation. While the shape and size of your site may restrict the way the building is placed, assuming that you have a relatively level site and it is of such a shape that you can place the building however you want to, there are a few general statements that can be made.

The building should be located longitudinally on an east-west axis. In the National Archives' East Burwood facility, the staffing areas were placed on the eastern end of the building to capitalise on the morning sun, with the storage areas located at the rear. In Australia, where the climate is cool for a large part of the year, more of a building's northern aspect can be used for staffing and the general public. Given that the northern and western walls of your storage areas will thus bear the impact of the sun, you will need to take this into account with respect to wall insulation and internal air distribution.

You should also pay particular attention to the direction from which the prevailing winds originate and whether they are hot or cold, dry or moist. This too will have an impact on insulation and internal air distribution. For example, if the prevailing winds are moist and your storage areas face those winds, then the insulation will need to reduce the possibility of moisture migrating through the walls and into the storage areas. Prevailing wind direction should also be noted in the context of the building's principal air intakes. They should be placed on the opposite side. This helps reduce the level of pollution entering the building's airconditioning system. When locating the main driveway and parking areas, you should remember to allow for turning circles for large delivery vehicles and should allow for an appropriate number of parking spaces for both staff and visitors. Remember too, that the fire brigade may need access to all parts of the building's exterior, should you ever have an emergency situation, and, if your building is set well back from the street, there needs to be sufficient room to allow vehicles unrestricted access.

Last, if you are in a residential area and your building is going to be a large one, plan to have the building blend into its surroundings as much as possible, rather than detract from them. In this context, when building its Runcorn facility, the Queensland State Archives used residential housing as its model and produced a building with large overhanging eaves, a curved roof and exposed concrete columns reminiscent of stumps.[14] The design has helped to create a building that augments its surroundings.

At Runcorn, the Queensland State Archives used local housing as a model ensuring that it would blend into its residential surroundings.
Photograph courtesy of Queensland State Archives; reproduced by kind permission of Queensland State Archives.

Building upwards, outwards or down

Throughout the world archival institutions have constructed their buildings in a variety of ways. Some have built up – as the Public Records Office of Hong Kong have done at Kwun Tong. Their new building is 10 storeys high.

Some have built outwards in a modular fashion – as the Archives Office of New South Wales have done at Kingswood. As the need arises a new module is added, being connected to earlier modules.

Some have built underground as the Riksarkivet, Sweden, have done in Stockholm; a six-storey storage facility wih a capacity of 100 kilometres, completed in 1968. And some have built into the sides of mountains as the archives of the Church of Jesus Christ of Latter-Day Saints in Utah, USA, have done. These latter examples have usually arisen as a form of protection against conventional warfare, or as protection against the threat of nuclear war which reached its peak during the Cold War of the 1950s and 1960s.

The Archives Office of New South Wales has built outwards in a modular fashion at Kingswood.
Photograph reproduced by kind permission of Archives Office of New South Wales.

Building upwards (multi-storeyed), outwards (modular) or down, (underground) – is there a right way? The short answer is no. In reality, it depends on the amount of land that you have available, other restrictions that might be imposed by the land (eg a severely sloping site) and the overall needs of your organisation. There are advantages and disadvantages whichever way you decide to build.

If a small site is available, building upwards may be the only option. In Hong Kong, the site of the new archives building is only 730 square metres and is surrounded by other buildings, including a church, hence building outwards was not an option. Building upwards, however, requires the added cost of deeper site excavation, stronger foundations and the costs of lifts and their maintenance.

Building outwards in an ever increasing fashion may appear to be an attractive option, seemingly able to guarantee you unlimited access to expansion. This option too is not without difficulties. First, extremely large tracts of land are required and in the initial stages only a small portion will be used. The Archives Office of New South Wales' Kingswood site is just over 22 hectares. Such land must be purchased at the outset otherwise it may not be available in the future. In addition to the high purchase price, there is the cost of maintaining the land, though this can be offset if the land can be sub-leased for other purposes and then resumed at a later stage. There are the costs of connecting services (such as airconditioning and power) to each new module and ensuring that each module is fully compatible with the ones built before it.

There is an additional disadvantage. Having a large volume of land, with portions set aside for future use, may give the appearance of under-utilisation of the site. This, in turn, could render you vulnerable to whichever cash-strapped government or business you belong if that government or business is seeking to dispose of surplus assets quickly. The land could be taken from you and disposed of, with the profits being dispersed elsewhere.

Building underground will certainly afford you protection from the risks of warfare. And it may offer very stable environmental conditions, if the surrounding rock surfaces are of the right type. But, again, there are disadvantages. First, there are the initial high costs of excavation. Unless you have access to an abandoned mineshaft or something similar, excavation costs are likely to be prohibitive. There are the added costs of insulation and the ever present risk of dampness caused by underground streams and springs.

In this context, it should be noted that the Riksarkivet, Sweden, completed a new facility in 1995. The Archives could not afford the cost of expanding its existing underground facility in Stockholm, and the new facility has been built above ground on a site 15 kilometres from the existing one.

Tanking

If the storage area of your facility is located below ground you can minimise the possibility of water ingress by using a series of construction techniques known as 'tanking'. The procedure is intended to prevent water rising up through the floor or passing through the walls from the outside. Basically, a waterproof membrane is located below the floor. A damp proof course is built into the perimeter walls. The walls themselves are treated to resist the passage of moisture (this process is described in detail in chapter 7). The membrane, damp proof course and the moisture seal should provide complete protection for the repository area. Should there be any water under the floor a series of drains can aid in its removal.

Arningedepan – Riksarkivet, National Archives of Sweden.
Photograph reproduced by kind permission of National Archives of Sweden.

In recent years, most institutions have adopted a compromise approach, using a combination of the upwards and outwards methods. A site is acquired which will allow for the construction of an initial facility two or three storeys high. The site is of sufficient size that one or possibly two extensions can be built at a future stage. The extensions can take the form of a second building joined to the first one, lengthening the original building, or adding another storey to the first building.

The compromise approach has been adopted by the National Archives at most of its facilities, including Villawood and East Burwood, and by the Queensland State Archives at Runcorn.

Whichever way you plan to expand in the future, you must ensure that your initial site selection and construction allows you to do this. If the ultimate aim is to expand upwards, the footings (foundations) of the initial building must be sufficient to take the weight of an additional storey. If the intention is to expand outwards, it may pay you to ensure that all site works are completed at the outset rather than in successive stages. The cost of bringing large earth-moving equipment onto a site is extraordinarily high and it may well be cost efficient to have this done in the one instance rather than in a piecemeal fashion. The site at East Burwood was prepared in this way, even though the building only occupies part of the area. The building was designed with an extension planned after a period of about 10 years and it was considered cost efficient to have all the site works done at the outset, rather than progressively.

The Building's Fabric

When contemplating the design of a purpose-built repository there is a general statement that should be made at the outset. What you should be seeking is an environment which will ensure the preservation of your valuable records. All elements of the building's fabric have a part to play in this – the walls, doors, roof and floors. They should all be designed to come together to form an integrated and sealed unit. By themselves each piece is insignificant, but joined together the picture becomes clearer in much the same way as the pieces of a jigsaw puzzle interlink to form a comprehensive picture.

If this is done correctly, what you will achieve is a 'total preservation environment'[15] which will ensure stable, or constant, environmental conditions. This single factor is now widely recognised and understood far more than previously.

In Canada, however, they have taken the concept a step further with the 'building within a building' approach to their overall layout. The National Archives of Canada adopted this method for their Gatineau facility.[16] The idea is that areas involving people, with regular movement in and out, are located as close to the outer shell of the building as possible, and the storage areas are located near the central 'heart' of the building. By this method, the storage areas are further protected from external climatic variations. The downside to this approach is that for most archives buildings storage will represent the great bulk of the total floor space. So you need to have a very large building – which Gatineau certainly is – in order to completely surround the storage area with office and public facilities. Second, the inclusion of inner storage walls adds to the overall construction cost.

In Germany and England, some institutions have pursued a different path whereby the building fabric has been used as the primary means of creating a stable environment. The principle is known as 'passive climate control' or 'thermal inertia'.[17] It involves the use of materials with strong thermal mass – in essence, a double cavity wall, with an air gap, and a more effective use of insulation. Airconditioning systems are generally not used, but heating and ventilation systems are. Thus it is claimed that appropriate environmental conditions are achieved and energy costs are low. Christoffersen reports success with this method, and, at first glance, the results are impressive. However, his results also show that throughout the year the internal temperature fluctuates from 14.5° Celsius to 20.5° Celsius and relative humidity levels between 56% and 62%.[18]

Given the high humidity levels in Australian coastal cities, the usefulness of relying solely on passive climate control must be called into question. The tendency in this country in recent years has been to adopt a compromise approach, to combine a sound building fabric together with an airconditioning system as the principal means of ensuring stable conditions.

When planning your building's structure, one of the things you need to decide at the outset is how large your individual storage areas should be. Specialised storage areas (including security and film vaults) will be considered in chapter 4, yet with respect to general storage there are two points that should be noted. First, large expanses of open storage make it difficult to control environmental conditions; second, they make it difficult to contain a fire.

In this context, mezzanine floors also make it difficult to maintain conditions. While they provide the boon of added storage capacity, they add to the overall open area that must be controlled. As an example of 1970s archival architecture, the Villawood facility has open floor areas over 3 400 square metres. Now, the trend is for much smaller areas. In the new Gatineau facility there are 48 storage areas where each is only 350 square metres. The new Kew building has 14 storage areas.

You should also be wary of pillars in the storage areas, particularly out in the open, as opposed to having them in corners or against the walls. It would be wise to advise the architect to keep them to a minimum. They impede the layout of shelving and consume valuable storage space. If there are pillars, they should have protective metal corners attached to them to prevent any damage by staff pushing heavily laden trolleys.

Walls

The walls of most modern repositories are generally made from bricks or concrete. Some facilities have single walls and others have double walls with a cavity in between. It should be noted that, given the right circumstances, bricks and concrete can both be porous and allow the passage of moisture from the outside, where humidity levels are generally higher, into the storage areas. So the walls should be designed and built in such a way as to minimise the potential for external environmental conditions to influence the conditions you are maintaining in the storage areas. This usually means the inclusion of a vapour barrier (see chapter 7 for a case study describing adding a vapour barrier to an existing building).

Bricks have been used in the construction of storage walls in a number of the National Archives' facilities. In some cases, the organisation has experienced problems with moisture penetration through these walls and has had to apply vapour proofing material as a means of overcoming these problems.

All walls which surround record storage areas should be fire rated. The term FRL (Fire Resistance Level) is often used in this context. Fire ratings consist of three numbers (eg 60/60/60). The numbers are in minutes and refer to:
- structural adequacy – the item will not collapse in that time;
- integrity – the item will not fail in that time, ie the fire will not burn through; and
- insulation – the ability of the item to withstand heat, both conducted and radiant.[19]

Fire ratings for walls and doors have not, however, been standardised. The 1977 version of British Standard (BS) 5454 recommended a four-hour rating, but in the revised 1989 edition this was deleted and no time period was specified.[20] Duchein recommends two hours,[21] as does DIS 11799: 1998.[22]

The National Archives recommends a period of two hours, but uses this rating in conjunction with sprinklers which are found in all of its facilities. Conversely, the Archives Office of New South Wales has adopted a four-hour rating at Kingswood, applying this rating to those parts of the facility that do not have sprinklers.

The National Archives of Singapore has combined both of these parameters at Canning Rise and applied a four-hour rating, as well as installing sprinklers.

Doors

All doors leading into the storage areas should be solid and should also be fire rated, the same rating applying to the walls.

The doors should also be designed and built to create an effective seal when closed. If there are gaps around the doors or frames, then the 'bleeding' effect will result in the loss of internal environmental conditions. Doors which face the building's exterior should be weather proofed.

Doors should naturally be large enough to permit the movement of trolleys laden with boxes. If doors are subject to regular use by staff pushing trolleys, it would be a wise move to have protective metal strips placed across the lower half on both sides.

Roofs

Roofs are generally built from tiles or steel. The Public Record Office of the United Kingdom has used slate tiles for its new building at Kew. The National Archives has used terracotta tiles for a number of its facilities. Tiles, whether slate or terracotta, are attractive and waterproof, though they can be costly. Most repositories have steel roofs. If steel is the preferred choice, then it must be treated to ensure it is rust proofed.

Whatever your roof is made of, you should remember that heat will radiate through it. So sufficient room needs to be allowed within the roof cavity for ventilation. The roof cavity should also be insulated to prevent heat transfer into your storage areas.

Experience over the past 25 years has shown that the roof should be well sealed, not only to keep out rain and wind, but to prohibit the entry of birds and other pests.

At Kew, the Public Record Office of the United Kingdom has used slate tiles on the roof which, though waterproof and attractive, can be costly.
Photograph by John Critchley; reproduced by his permission.

The roof should be pitched and at such a level as to ensure rapid rainwater run-off. Flat roofs should be avoided. The Villawood repository has a flat roof and, over the years, there have been frequent problems with water penetration. In the longer term it will probably require replacement. The Archives Office of New South Wales' Kingswood repository experienced similar problems with a flat roof, and a new, pitched roof has since been installed over the top of the older one.

Roof penetrations should be kept to an absolute minimum. Apart from smoke exhaust systems (which will be discussed in chapter 3), there is little need for other forms of roof penetration. The more roof penetrations there are, the greater will be the risk of leaks. In essence, water-tight integrity of the storage areas is paramount.

Drainage

The building's drainage system should be designed to quickly remove water not only from the building, but from the property as well. Gutters and down pipes should be designed to ensure water collected does not overflow back into the building. In this context, box gutters should be avoided because, as they are located inside the building and not externally, there is the potential for water to leak straight into the storage areas.

You should be wary of large trees, particularly those of the eucalyptus variety, which drop leaves, bark and twigs onto the roof and can block your guttering and downpipes. Their roots can also interfere with drainage systems. It is wise not to have such trees near the building.

The building should not have internal drain pipes. The National Archives' facility at Mitchell in north Canberra has internal drain pipes and there has long been the inherent risk of leakage, not to mention noise disturbance to staff, during periods of heavy rainfall.

There should be sufficient drainage channels on the site itself to remove water quickly. This is really what it is all about – removing water from the building, and then from the property, as rapidly as possible.

Windows and skylights

The issue of having windows and skylights in record storage areas is a vexed question. They have been discussed by a number of writers[23] and, as with so many aspects of building management, there is no general agreement.

A number of older Australian archival facilities have windows in their storage areas, eg the National Archives' buildings at Villawood, Mitchell, East Victoria Park (Western Australia) and Rosny Park (Tasmania). Yet most modern facilities, including East Burwood and Runcorn, do not.

The answer to this dilemma is deceptively simple. Storage areas are for records, not people. Records, no matter what their value or retention period may be, do not require a view. Further, direct sunlight (even if filtered glass is used) is going to have a deleterious effect on records preservation. So, there is no place for windows in storage areas.

There is no place for skylights in storage areas either. Apart from the issue of allowing the passage of sunlight, a skylight simply represents another roof penetration and brings with it the risk of roof leaks during periods of heavy rainfall.

It may be argued that large storage areas with expanses of mobile shelving can have a demoralising effect on staff and the view from windows, or the light from a skylight, can alleviate this problem. There are alternatives to windows and skylights to ensure that a storage area has an aesthetically pleasing impact, eg the use of framed prints or posters around the walls and even decorative panels on the entrance to each row of shelving.

Floors and ceilings

As with walls, the floors and ceilings should be designed to minimise the potential for external conditions influencing the conditions being maintained in storage areas.

False ceilings are often provided for cosmetic reasons. They serve as a means of concealing airconditioning trunking and the underside of the floor above. Essential services, such as lighting, airconditioning vents and sprinkler heads, are attached to the false ceiling.

Regardless of whether a false ceiling is used or not, during the initial design phase careful consideration must be given to the floor-to-ceiling height separation in the storage areas. British Standard (BS) 5454 states that 2 600 mm[24] is the minimum height needed, but depending on how high the shelving is, and whether sprinklers are likely to be installed, this figure could be grossly inadequate.

The determining factor is, of course, how high the shelving is going to be. But other factors come into play. Mobile shelving (which is discussed in chapter 4) can be supplied in a number of standard heights. In addition to the actual shelving, there are the bases underneath and these will add another 180 mm or so to the overall height. If raised tracks (rather than below ground tracks) are to be used, this will add another 50 mm.

Last, if sprinklers are to be installed, there is a requirement for 500 mm clearance between the top of the shelving units and the sprinkler heads, in accordance with Australian Standard 2118.1-1995 *Automatic Fire Sprinkler Systems*.[25] The use of sprinklers is an emotive issue and will be considered in more detail in chapter 3.

So, for example, if you are using the National Archives' standard shelving height of 2 475 mm, then add the 180 mm height of the bases and the 500 mm clearance required for the sprinklers, the overall floor-to-ceiling height will be 3 155 mm. Now, if raised tracks are to be used, then about another 50 mm would need to be added.

Floors are generally made from reinforced concrete. If the building is located in an area prone to high humidity levels, it may be necessary for a water-proof membrane to be laid below the floor to prevent moisture penetration from below.

It is preferable that the floors be covered. The most ideal covering is vinyl, either tiles or in sheet form. Bare concrete is not recommended, but if it must be used it should be sealed, otherwise it is likely to give off contaminants which can affect the records, the airconditioning system and possibly staff working in the area.

Carpets and 'spongy' vinyl should not be used in storage areas. Put simply, carpet – even the industrial strength variety – will be destroyed by heavily laden trolleys frequently passing over it. Incidentally, shelving tracks should never be installed directly over carpet or spongy tiles as the 'give' may cause the tracks to deflect.

Floor loadings

When fully laden, mobile shelving can accommodate extraordinary weights over a very small floor area. For a typical repository, each square metre of floor space can house 12 shelf metres of records if they are stored in mobile shelving eight shelves in height. These records will weigh about 500–600 kilogrammes. To this must be added the weight of the shelving itself and the fact that the shelving moves which exerts extra pressure. Obviously, the floor must be capable of withstanding this pressure.[26]

Floor loadings are expressed in terms of kilopascals (kpa) which is a measure of pressure over a given area. It is a requirement of the National Archives that storage areas should have a floor loading of at least 12 kpa if mobile shelving 2 475 mm high (8 shelves) is used. This equates to a tolerance of just over 1.2 tonnes per square metre. The loading will vary considerably if higher or lower installations are to be used.

For office areas, the loadings are much less. Normally a loading of only 5 kpa (0.510 tonnes per square metre) will be sufficient. If there is any doubt about floor loadings, the advice of a structural engineer should be sought.

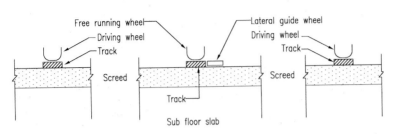

Three track above ground installation.
Drawing by John de Salis of the National Archives of Australia.

Shelving tracks

Mobile shelving operates on tracks which can either be installed above ground or below ground. If the building is new, then below ground tracks are commonly used and are installed as part of the overall construction process.

Generally, they can be laid two ways. They may be laid on the floor slab with concrete screed then being applied and levelled to a height of 3 mm below the top of the tracks. The 3 mm gap allows for the application of vinyl floor coverings which should finish flush with the tracks.

Another option is to rebate the floor slab as it is being poured. Rebates (sometimes referred to as 'chases') are longitudinal channels set in the floor. The tracks are then installed inside the rebates.

Tracks can be placed above ground, on small concrete mounts, usually about 50 mm high. In such cases, it is often a requirement that a false floor or ramp be provided to cover them, otherwise they impede the movement of trolleys and may actually present a hazard to staff. If a false floor or ramp is to be installed, it should be done after the tracks have been laid but before the shelving is installed.

If below ground tracks are being used, it is imperative that the architect and the builder both understand that overall floor levels are critical to the smooth operation of mobile shelving.

Floor levels around building pillars can sometimes be slightly uneven, being caused by 'back-wash' when the screed is poured, and this in turn may lead to the grounding of mobile shelving units. This has been a common problem at Villawood.

Loading docks

Naturally, a purpose-built facility will require the delivery of new records and maybe the temporary withdrawal of existing ones. To this end, vehicular access will be required and a loading dock of sufficient size will be needed. Loading docks may appear a simple matter, but errors in their design can often cause major problems in the future.

First, loading docks should be designed to allow large vehicles to fit inside them and thus protect records during the transfer stage. This may sound blindingly obvious, but it has not always been done this way.

If the floor of the dock is sloping, it should be away from the building, not towards it. If the floor slopes downwards towards the building, rainwater will run down and into the facility. Even with good drainage inside the dock, this is a problem that careful planning at the outset will avoid.

Loading docks should be sealed off from storage areas by means of airlocks. Docks should never open directly onto a storage area. Otherwise you are faced with the problem whereby a vehicle reverses into the dock with its engine running and carbon monoxide and other pollutants gain access to the storage areas. Similarly, while the storage doors are opened, the environmental conditions which you have struggled so hard to attain, and at considerable energy costs, are lost to the outside world.

You should also consider how you are going to transfer records to and from vehicles in the dock. A fixed platform at the rear of the dock, or some other form of adjustable platform, sometimes called a 'dock leveller', will be very useful.

Once clear of the loading dock, the airlock should open directly onto the storage areas so that persons pushing heavily laden trolleys have easy access and do not have to negotiate tight corners.

Plant rooms

Plant rooms should be designed to allow not only the installation of large items of plant – such as boilers and chillers – but also their removal at a later stage. Given that the average repository will have a minimum life span of 50 years, all items of plant will eventually reach the end of their working life and will require replacement. This usually occurs within 20 years. Obviously, this will necessitate their removal from the building, so ready access to the plant room will be needed to permit this.

The plant room's external entrance should have large doors and provision should be made for an access road connecting the room to the main road.

Principal air intakes

You should carefully note where the facility's principal air intakes are to be located. It is preferable that they should not be located on the side of the building that faces prevailing winds, and certainly not on the side of the building which faces any nearby industries likely to produce pollutants. Last, the air intakes should never be located in a carpark. Otherwise all the carbon monoxide produced by the vehicles using the park will be pulled into the airconditioning system contaminating the filters. If the air intakes are poorly located, the best filtration systems available will be of little use in keeping out the pollutants.

Room for control panels

In later chapters, reference will be made to the need for fire and security panels and possibly an emergency warning and intercommunication system. If your building has these facilities, they will all be located in the foyer. They must all be readily accessible. Indeed, there is a legal requirement that the fire panel be accessible to the fire brigade.

While they are necessary, these panels can be unsightly and an inconvenience to your staff and visitors to your building, particularly when they are undergoing regular maintenance inspections. It is a good idea to have a small room adjacent to the foyer where all these panels can be installed and thus not present a hindrance.

Environmental issues

Environmental issues were basically non-existent when older repositories were designed and built. Prior to building its Villawood repository, the National Archives had first to obtain approval from the Parliamentary Standing Committee on Public Works, the Government agency which endorses such projects. The word 'environment' never appeared in submissions made to the Committee either by the Archives or the Department of Works, nor in the Committee's own final report.[27]

Today, however, archivists are responsible for managing 'green' buildings. Most government agencies are expected to include an environmental impact statement as part of their proposals for new works. When preparing its brief for East Burwood in 1991, the National Archives was required to seek input from its parent Department, as well as the Australian Heritage Commission. And on this occasion, in its final report, the Parliamentary Standing Committee on Public Works noted the minimal environmental impact the project would have.[28]

Environmental issues can range from the impact your building will have on its surrounds, energy management and the use of chloro-fluorocarbons (CFCs), particularly in older buildings.

Purpose-built repositories with airconditioning plants operating constantly and possessing large expanses of lighting are, of course, significant users of power. The challenge has been to use existing energy sources wisely and, obviously, to use less energy. A number of measures have been developed to meet this challenge.

Again, the materials that will comprise your building's fabric are important. There has been a considerable increase in the use of more efficient insulative materials. Creating a sealed environment in the storage areas helps in this regard. Even simple measures, such as ensuring there are no leaks around door frames which will let conditioned air escape, are now widely put into effect. Other measures have included detailed studies of energy tariffs and whether cheaper tariffs are available from the electricity supplier and the controlled use of lighting in storage areas.

The recent introduction of building management systems (which will be discussed in more detail in chapter 3) have played their part too. They enable a more efficient control of airconditioning plants than was the case before.

In recent times, much has been said about other forms of energy, including solar and wind power. To date, they have had little impact on repository design, though certainly there is a place for solar systems to provide hot water for rest rooms and amenities areas. It may well be that repositories in the next century will make greater use of alternative energy supplies to power the facility in its entirety.

Chloro-fluorocarbons (CFCs) are present in many older repositories in three ways. The first two form part of the building's fire protection – halon gas flood systems (BTM 1301) and hand-held extinguishers (BCF 1211). The third is in the form of chiller refrigerants R11 or R12. In Australia there has been a requirement that all halon systems, both BTM and BCF, be removed from service by 1 January 1996 unless a certificate of exemption has been granted.[29]

At present, there is no set date for the phasing out of refrigerants R11 and R12. However, their import to Australia is no longer permitted and institutions which use these refrigerants will gradually find it more and more difficult to keep the systems in service.

1   Georg Winter, 'Gedanken ueber einen Archiv-Neubau', *Archivum*, vol. VI, 1956, pp. 93–99.
2   Victor Gondos, 'Archival buildings – programming and planning', *American Archivist*, vol. 27, no. 4, 1964, p. 468.
3   Robert Sharman, 'New building for old. The transmigration of the Queensland State Archives', *Archives and Manuscripts*, vol. 3, no. 7, 1968, p. 25.
4   Michael Saclier, 'Buildings for archives and public records', *Proceedings of the 16th Biennial Conference of the Library Association of Australia* held in Sydney, August 1971, p. 241.
5   National Archives (ACT): A750, General correspondence files, annual single number series, item 1964/147, ff. 22–23.
6   A750, item 1964/147, f. 58.
7   A750, item 1969/246, ff. 28–29.
8   A750, item 1969/246, f. 155.
9   National Archives, *Functional Brief for the Construction of a Purpose Built Repository for National Archives Victoria*, Melbourne, 1991.
10 A750, item 1964/147, f. 53.
11 Specific examples of such literature include: Lionel Bell, 'Archival accommodation in the United Kingdom', *Journal of the Society of Archivists*, vol. 6, no. 6, 1980, pp. 352–357; Michel Duchein, *Archive Buildings and Equipment*, Munich, 1988, pp. 29–31; Jay Haymond, 'Adaptive reuse of old buildings for archives', *American Archivist*, vol. 45, no. 1, 1982, pp. 11–18; Christopher Kitching, *Archive Buildings in the United Kingdom 1977–1992*, London, 1993, pp. 53–59; Peter Pavel Klasinc, 'Archival functions and the adaptation of existing buildings for archival needs', *Atlanti*, 5, 1995, pp. 101–105; and Irena G Shepilova and Adrienne G Thomas, *Main principles of fire protection in libraries and archives: A RAMP study*, Paris, 1992, pp. 12–13 (fire safety aspects only).
    A collection of articles will also be found in the International Council on Archives 'Proceedings of the 1989 meeting of ICA/CBQ on the adaptation of existing buildings for archival needs', *Janus*, 1992.1, pp. 49–86.
12 A750, item 1964/147, ff. 61–82.
13 The problems associated with halons and other unfriendly products will be discussed briefly in chapter 3.
14 Vicki Warden, 'The new Queensland State Archives building', paper presented to the Conference of the Australian Society of Archivists, Townsville, May 1994, p. 49.
15 Vicki Warden, verbal quote to the author, August 1994.
16 Jean-Pierre Wallot, *The Archivist*, number 114, 1997, p. 2.
17 There are a number of sources which discuss this principle, eg: Wolf Buchmann, 'Preservation: buildings and equipment', paper presented to the 5th European Conference on Archives, Barcelona, May 1997, pp. 8–13; Lars D Christoffersen, *Zephyr Passive Climate Controlled Repositories Storage Facilities for Museum, Archive and Library Purposes*, Lund, 1995; Christopher Kitching, *Archive Buildings in the United Kingdom 1977–1992*, pp. 20–22; and Sandra Rowoldt, 'The greening of archive buildings: natural airconditioning in the Southern African context', *Janus*, 1993.2, pp. 36–41.
18 Lars D Christoffersen, pp. 61–62.
19 Australian Building Codes Board, *Building Code of Australia*, Canberra, 1996, page 2 054 and verbal advice provided by Mr Brian Hay, Senior Officer (Technical) with the Secretariat of the Commonwealth Fire Board, Melbourne.
20 British Standard (BS) 5454, *Recommendations for Storage and Exhibition of Archival Documents*, London, 1989, p. 4.
21 Michel Duchein, *Archive Buildings and Equipment*, p. 97.
22 International Standards Organisation ISO/TC46/SC10 *Information and Documentation/Physical keeping of Documents* DIS 11799: 1998 *Information and Documentation – Storage Requirements for Archive and Library Materials*, Copenhagen, 1998, p. 5.
23 Christopher Kitching, *Archive Buildings in the United Kingdom 1977–1992*, pp. 28–30; Michel Duchein, *Archive Buildings and Equipment*, pp. 47–48; Wolf Buchmann, paper presented to the European Conference on Archives 1977, p. 14.
24 British Standard (BS) 5454, p. 3.
25 Australian Standard 2118.1-1995, *Automatic Fire Sprinkler Systems*, Sydney, 1995, p. 56.
26 The figures given are averages only. They will vary depending on the height of the shelving and the nature of records being stored within.
27 Parliamentary Standing Committee on Public Works, Canberra, 1970.
28 Parliamentary Standing Committee on Public Works, *Report relating to the Construction of a New Permanent Repository for National Archives at East Burwood, Vic.*, Parliamentary Paper 83 of 1992, p. 23.
29 Commonwealth Fire Board Fire Safety Circular 91, p. 1 and brochures produced by the Environment Protection Group.

Chapter 3
Inside the Building

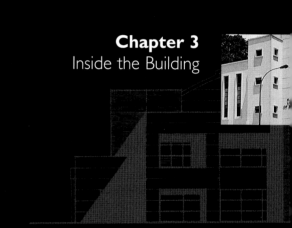

EAST

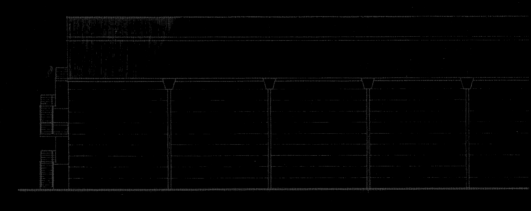

SOUTH

Having considered the building's structure, the next step is to look at how a building functions on the inside.

Earlier it was stated that one of the key roles of a purpose-built repository is the preservation of records. In order to achieve this, you will need to establish and maintain strict environmental conditions throughout your building. And you need to ensure that the building has appropriate levels of fire and security protection.

Creating the Right Conditions

There are four questions that must now be addressed:
- why are environmental conditions so important for records protection?
- what are the right environmental conditions?
- how are these conditions achieved?
- how do you actually monitor these conditions?

Why are environmental conditions so important?

In recent times, the impact of environmental conditions on record formats has been studied by a number of archivists and conservators.[1] There are four criteria which can be grouped under this banner – temperature, relative humidity, air quality and light.

Temperature and relative humidity

Records are created in many physical formats. Each format usually involves a combination of components which in some cases occur naturally and in others are manufactured. These components can react differently to environmental extremes. As a result, each record format usually has its own set of preservation requirements. Conditions that are ideal for paper preservation will not be the same for film or magnetic tape.

Paper mostly comprises cellulose fibres derived from plants. Chemical additives are also used which help improve its writing quality, appearance and longevity. These components can be very responsive to changes in temperature and relative humidity. For example, if humidity levels are too high, paper will absorb moisture and you are likely to see mould growth. If levels are too low, the fibres dry out and become brittle.[2]

Photographic film consists of a thin, light sensitive layer coated on a clear plastic base. Over the years a number of products have been used as the base, eg cellulose nitrate, cellulose acetate and polyester. Film, like paper, reacts to environmental extremes. The image-bearing layer can separate from the base, or the film can become brittle. Images can fade or stain. Cellulose nitrate degrades over time releasing nitric acid which can affect other records around it. Of even greater danger is the fact that films made from this base can self ignite. Cellulose acetate, which replaced nitrate film in the 1950s, can release acetic acid as it degrades, a process commonly known as 'vinegar syndrome'.[3]

Magnetic tape consists of a polyester base, a binder system on one side of the tape and magnetic oxide particles embedded in the binder. Chemical reactions affecting the tape increase with rises in temperature and relative humidity. One effect is that the binder layer breaks down.[4]

The influence of temperature and relative humidity holds true for other formats too, including photographs and gramophone recordings.

TABLE 3 PARAMETERS FOR THE STORAGE OF PAPER, AUDIOVISUAL AND MAGNETIC MEDIA

Source	Paper (°C/Rel Hum%)	B/W Film (°C/Rel Hum%)	Magnetic Media (°C/Rel Hum%)
Michel Duchein[5]	18/55	12/35	18/40
Arnold den Teuling[6]	16-18/50-55	5-18/30-40	18/40
William K Wilson[7]	15/50	Not stated	Not stated
BS 5454[8]	13-18/55-65	Not stated	4-16/40-60
DIS 11799: 1998[9]	18/50	21/50	20/40
National Archives[10]	20/50	18/35	18/35

In general terms, all materials degrade over time and, following basic principles of chemistry, the more energy that goes into a chemical reaction, then the faster that reaction will proceed. In this context, heat, moisture and light are all contributing factors, so with lower temperature, humidity and light levels, degradation will be slowed. However, the need to retard the degradation process must be balanced against human requirements and the environmental conditions at which records will be accessible.

What are the right environmental conditions?

There is actually no strict answer to this question. Despite copious research, there is yet to emerge a universally accepted set of 'correct' environmental conditions. Though, as research has intensified, one fact that is widely acknowledged is that recommended levels, or 'set points', have gradually been decreasing.

What has been recognised and accepted for some time is that constant temperature and relative humidity levels can greatly assist records protection, irrespective of their format. Frequent fluctuations in either temperature or humidity will only hasten records degradation. Whatever environmental levels you adopt, these conditions should be monitored 24 hours a day and any deviations should be noted and acted upon. If a pattern of drift is established, even within set tolerances, action should be taken to return to stable conditions. The critical factor here is that conditions must not simply be created, they must be *constantly sustained*.

Strict controls should apply in all areas where permanent value records are held – not only the storage areas, but conservation laboratories and other locations, even if the records are only held there on a temporary basis.

Recent publications have provided a range of parameters for the storage of paper, audiovisual material and magnetic media.

These figures clearly demonstrate that there are still some widely divergent opinions with no accepted standards.

The picture has been clouded even further with the 1994 release of a series of reports by the Smithsonian Institute – Conservation Analytical Laboratory.[11] The authors indicate that it may not be necessary to adopt a range of stringently regulated parameters as record formats may not be affected by major variations in conditions after all. Such statements are, of course, completely at odds with more widely held views and the reports have not settled the debate. The controversy is just as strong as ever.

Until the debate is resolved, you should adopt a series of set points for each record format. For paper, it is suggested that between 18° and 20° Celsius and 50% humidity are appropriate. Conditions should then be monitored closely and should not be allowed to deviate from these set points for any length of time. The aim should always be the maintenance of conditions which, if placed on a graph, would closely resemble a horizontal line.

The table on page 46 shows what other archival institutions have adopted as their environmental parameters for paper and film storage:

TABLE 4 CURRENT EXAMPLES OF ENVIRONMENTAL CONDITIONS FOR RECORD STORAGE

Facility	Institution	Paper (°C/Rel Hum%)	B/W film (°C/Rel Hum%)	Colour film (°C/Rel Hum%)
Villawood	National Archives	20/50	10/35	n/a
East Burwood	National Archives	18/50	10/35	n/a
Kingswood	Archives Office of New South Wales	21/50-55	20/45	n/a
Runcorn	Queensland State Archives	20/50	18/40	n/a
Berriedale	Archives Office of Tasmania	18-20/50	18/30-40	n/a
Portside	BHP Pty Ltd	18/50	18/50	n/a
Wellington	National Archives of New Zealand	19/50	11/50	n/a
Nouville	Archives Territoriales, New Caldeonia	18-20/55	12/35	n/a
College Park	National Archives and Records Administration, USA	21/45	18/30	minus 4/30
Gatineau	National Archives of Canada	18/40	18/25	minus 18/25
Kew	Public Record Office, UK	17/55	17/40	n/a
Koblenz	Bundesarchiv, Germany	18/50	13/50	minus 6/25
Arningedepan	Riksarkivet, Sweden	18/40	n/a	n/a
Ulleval Hageby	Riksarkivet, National Archives of Norway	20/50	10/23	n/a
Beijing	Beijing Municipal Archives	15-24/60-65	18/40	n/a
Shanghai	Shanghai Municipal Archives	18-22/50-60	12-20/40-50	n/a
Kwun Tong	Public Records Office, Hong Kong	18/45	14/35	n/a
Taejon	Government Archives and Records Service, Republic of Korea	20/45	10/40	n/a
Canning Rise	National Archives of Singapore	18/50	15/40	n/a

As shown by the table, very few institutions have a dedicated colour film storage area. The preservation of colour film requires even more stringent conditions than for black and white film; the reason being the dyes or pigments used in the film which can fade over time. Most institutions simply rely on their black and white film storage area for colour film preservation.

To provide you with further guidance, the National Archives has produced a series of charts entitled *Guidelines for Environmental Conditions and Safety and Protection Levels for Storage*. The charts summarise conditions which the Archives believes are necessary for the protection of records in varying formats both over and less than 30 years of age. They are issued to government agencies throughout Australia. Copies of both charts are at the end of this book at Appendices 1 and 2 respectively.

Air quality

When considering environmental conditions, there is sometimes a tendency to focus solely on temperature and relative humidity levels. These are clearly important but, as was indicated earlier, there are two other criteria that must not be forgotten. The first of these is air quality.

The air which passes through the building has an important role to play in records preservation. This air should be kept in continuous motion day and night, being recirculated to all parts of the facility. The air must also be filtered. Air entering the building can contain contaminants such as dust, sulphur dioxide and carbon monoxide. The air inside the building can be polluted too. The records you are trying to protect can release contaminants as they deteriorate and people using the facility can do likewise, eg body odour. Whatever filtration system you use, it should be capable of removing the bulk of these, and other, impurities. There should also be a regular intake of fresh air. In areas which are staffed regularly the level would be set at 10%, but in storage areas the level can be less.

If the air is affected by pollutants or becomes stagnant, even if 'correct' conditions are maintained, you will achieve little. Acknowledgment of good filtration is not new; it was recognised by the Parliamentary Standing Committee on Public Works in its report for the National Archives' proposed Villawood facility as far back as 1970.[12]

Light

The second environmental criteria is light or, to be more precise, ultraviolet light which is found in natural light and can also emanate from some light fittings. Ultraviolet light too can have a detrimental effect on records, whatever their format.

For this reason, natural light should not be allowed to enter the storage areas, regardless of whether these areas house permanent or temporary value records. To reiterate the comments made in chapter 2, storage areas are for the preservation of records which do not require a view of the surrounding countryside. If you must have windows, you should use ultraviolet filtering film to help reduce the harmful effects created by the light.

To guard against the effects of ultraviolet light inside the building you can place filters over each light fitting, or you can use fittings which emit low ultraviolet light. The latter is preferable. Ultraviolet light has a wavelength less than 400 nanometres so your lights should emit a wavelength higher than this level. You can measure the level of ultraviolet light with a light meter. The levels are expressed in terms of microwatts per lumen. The accepted preservation limit is 75 microwatts per lumen.[13]

All light fittings should be covered with diffusers. They reduce the glare and help to spread the light more evenly.

How are the right conditions achieved?

In chapter 2, reference was made to the need for creating a sealed environment using the building's fabric. The designs of modern Australian repositories reflect this strategy and incorporate some common sense practices. You should regulate access into the storage areas; the greater the movement of people through these areas, the more you are likely to lose the conditions you are trying to achieve. Coupled with the philosophy of a sealed environment is the inclusion of an airconditioning and filtration system. This strategy will ensure that conditions remain stable and storage areas will be protected from the intrusion of contaminants.

It must be admitted that airconditioning systems often represent the bane of the archivist's life. If there is one factor that must be right from the earliest design phase and yet one that is often wrong, it is airconditioning systems. Even with today's technological wizardry, using them to achieve appropriate environmental conditions can sometimes be a difficult task. Architects and builders must be made to appreciate the conditions you are trying to achieve and the simple fact that these conditions must remain constant 24 hours a day.

How an airconditioning system actually works, and the components which make up the system, will be discussed shortly.

Monitoring environmental conditions

There are a number of ways of checking that the designated environmental conditions are being achieved. First, there are simple devices such as sling psychrometers and hand held probes. They are reasonably accurate, if calibrated correctly, though they require you to walk around the building recording conditions as you go. In essence, they are really used for 'spot checking' rather than as a form of regular monitoring.

Thermohygrographs are probably the most widely known measuring device, used by archives, libraries, museums and art galleries. As they are quite accurate they are a useful tool, again if calibrated correctly. However, they can only record conditions over a small area. To obtain a complete picture of conditions throughout a large part of the building, it will be necessary to install a number of devices. Having recorded the desired information, someone must collect, collate and analyse the results.

Yet being aware of conditions in one part of a facility is, in reality, quite limiting. It may be that conditions in that part are satisfactory but the remainder are not. What is really needed is a composite picture of conditions over the entire storage area. The most sophisticated, yet admittedly most expensive, method of achieving such a wide level of monitoring is with a building management system, or BMS.

These systems have appeared in recent years and have made a dramatic impact on building management; probably more so than any other form of technological change. With its wide array of sensors the BMS has a major advantage over other forms of monitoring. It can record conditions on an ongoing basis with minimal effort on your part. Further, when fully integrated with your airconditioning system, it can make adjustments when conditions stray outside designated parameters, or at least alert you that conditions have strayed.

All of these devices, however, record environmental conditions at the macro level. They show you what is occurring across an entire storage area, a floor, room, row of shelving or even an individual shelf. They cannot tell you about micro environmental conditions, ie what is occurring *inside* the record container, film canister or plan cabinet.[14] The sheer size of monitoring equipment, such as thermohygrographs, has generally precluded this from being done except for the very largest types of containers.

With the advent of portable electronic dataloggers over the past decade it is possible for micro conditions to be extensively monitored too. There are several such devices available which are small enough to fit inside most containers. They are usually battery powered and can record conditions at predetermined intervals for a considerable period of time – a week, month or even a year. The information can then be readily downloaded via computer for further analysis.

No doubt in the future, dataloggers operating in tandem with building management systems will help provide you with a more comprehensive picture of the conditions you are achieving. It is still too early to predict the outcome, but it is possible we may learn that micro conditions remain stable even when macro conditions begin to fluctuate. If this is the case, it could herald a re-thinking of designated macro parameters.

Components of an Airconditioning System

As was explained earlier, the preservation of all records, regardless of their format, is largely dependent on defined levels of temperature and relative humidity and the constant sustainment of these levels, coupled with a regular supply of filtered air. Most Australian institutions use airconditioning systems of one type or another to help them maintain their designated conditions and, in addition, to remove contaminants from the air as it is used in the building.

How an airconditioning system works

There are many different types of airconditioning systems and in a book such as this it is only intended to give a very generalised account.[15]

A quantity of outside air is drawn into the building through the principal air intake. It passes through a primary filter – usually a screen designed to catch debris, leaves, and even birds – through some ducting and enters at least one air handling unit. It is then mixed with air returning from the storage and other areas.

Most large buildings will require more than one air handling unit. Further, specialised storage areas, such as those dedicated to audiovisual materials, usually have their own designated unit due to the stricter set points they require.

A typical air handling unit will comprise a number of components, ie filters, cooling coil, supply air fan and dampers.

Filters

Contaminants in the air are removed by a series of filters within the air handling unit. There are many different types of filters available today and they are often referred to by collective titles including panel, bag, absorbant and electrostatic:

- Panel filters (sometimes called rock filters) consist of a bank of screens resembling fine mesh and are designed to trap larger sized contaminants. They are often pleated to increase the surface area of the filter media. The screens can be washed and reused or disposed of.
- Bag filters (also referred to as pocket filters) can also be arrayed in banks and are made from a combination of paper and fibre and are designed to trap very fine contaminants.
- Absorbant filters, as the name suggests, absorb extremely fine contaminants. When they have reached their saturation point they are disposed of. An example of this type of filter is activated charcoal.
- Electrostatic filters are designed to trap particles by means of electrical charges, the particles attaching themselves to the filter. Electrostatic filters are generally the most expensive type of filter.

It is usually the case that there will be a series of different filter types – two or three – each designed to trap or absorb contaminants on a sliding scale, large to small, as they pass through the system.

Depending on their type, filters may require either regular cleaning, washing or ultimate replacement. If this does not happen, their efficiency will be severely impaired and the air flowing through the system will be contaminated. In fact, under extreme circumstances, the filters can breakdown and release collected contaminants.

Cooling coil

The now mostly purified air passes through a cooling coil which, depending upon the cooling or dehumidification demand, can be cooled to a very low temperature, sometimes as low as 8° or 9° Celsius. This, of course, has the desired effect of reducing the air's temperature and moisture content. The water which forms as a by-product of the cooling process condenses on the coil, is collected and drained away.

Chiller

The means for cooling the coils in large airconditioning systems is usually provided by a water chiller which operates on a refrigeration cycle. The chilled water produced is pumped to the coil by means of piping. A valve regulates the flow of water. The chiller is not part of the handling unit itself but is normally located close to it.

Chiller refrigerants

In recent times the most commonly used chiller refrigerants have been R11 or R12. Both of these are chloro-fluorocarbons (CFCs) and, given their ozone depletion potential, are now being phased out.

Modern cooling systems use refrigerants commonly referred to as R22 or R134a. The former is a HCFC (hydrochloro-fluorocarbon) and is destined to be phased out early next century, whereas the latter is a HFC (hydrofluorocarbon), has no ozone depletion potential and no limit to its future use.

Supply air fan

Once the air has been filtered and conditioned to the nominated temperature and relative humidity levels, it is referred to as supply air. It leaves the air handling unit and travels through a series of ducts to the requisite parts of the building. In order to assist the process, a supply air fan helps keep the air moving.

The ductwork is insulated to prevent the air outside, which may have a higher heat or moisture content, from condensing on the ductwork's colder surfaces.

Dampers

Dampers are louvred devices located in both the air handling unit and the ductwork – in modern buildings they are usually motorised – which by opening and closing regulate the volume of air flowing throughout the entire system.

Humidifiers

If relative humidity levels of the conditioned air fall below the nominated set points during the cooling phase, this can be remedied by means of a steam humidifier which injects steam into the supply air. Humidifiers are normally located adjacent to the ducting.

Return air

The air which reaches the requisite areas within the building, and contributes to the maintenance of stable environmental conditions, must ultimately return. It leaves each area by means of return air grills, usually mounted on walls or ceilings, and enters a second set of ducting and flows back to the air handling unit. It is now referred to as *return air*. In larger buildings where there are systems which have lengthy ductwork, a return air fan may also be used to assist with the return of the air.

The air now returns to the handling unit and again mixes with more outside air. Odours and other contaminants which may have been picked up inside the building are removed after the introduction of this fresh outdoor air. The mixed air passes through the filtration system, then through the cooling coil once more, and the entire process thus repeats itself.

A quantity of stale air must also be exhausted from the building to equal the fresh air intake. If this did not occur, the build up of pressure would prevent fresh air entering. The removal is usually achieved by a series of dampers which regulate the exit of the stale air, though in some buildings there are openings through which the air is exhausted by means of positive pressure, eg opening of doors, gaps in window seals and the building fabric.

Heat release

One of the by-products of the airconditioning process is heat, eg the outside air may be 25° Celsius and inside the building it has been reduced to 20° Celsius. The heat which has been extracted from the air as it passes over the cooling coil must be removed from the system. This process is usually achieved by means of a cooling tower or air-cooled condensor, whereby the heat is piped to the tower or condensor before being dissipated to the atmosphere.

Cooling towers

Cooling towers, which are usually mounted on the roofs of buildings, have attracted considerable media attention in recent years following outbreaks of legionnaires' disease. The towers often provide the right mix of water and warm temperatures for the legionella bacteria to develop. For this reason, they are now subject to very strict maintenance requirements, which include regular dosing with biocides designed to destroy any possible bacteria build up.

Air-cooled condensors

Like cooling towers, they release heat into the atmosphere, but in this case the process uses air rather than water. As there is no water involved, legionella bacteria cannot develop.

Dehumidifiers

In some cases, dehumidifiers will also be included as part of the system. As the name suggests, they remove excess moisture from the air. They are particularly relevant for low temperature storage areas used for audiovisual materials where relative humidity levels of 35% may be required. They can also be used in tropical environments where external humidity levels can often be extremely high.

Heating

The process described so far involves the reduction of outside air temperature and relative humidity levels. There will, on occasion, be a requirement to raise the supply air temperature whenever the air outside the building is colder than that inside the building.

Heating can be achieved in one of two ways. First, as there is a cooling coil in the air handling unit, so too there can be a heating coil, located downstream from the cooling coil. Heating is supplied to the coil by means of an adjacent hot water boiler, which is usually gas powered. Second, a heating element can be located inside the ductwork, usually just beyond the air handling unit.

If heating is required, the air can either pass through, or bypass, the cooling coil – which is now not in operation – and then travels through the heating coil or the duct heater.

Airconditioning control systems

The monitoring of external and internal environmental conditions is a complicated process. So too is the overall regulation of the passage of air throughout a building.

In many buildings today, the entire process can now be monitored by means of a fully automated building management system (BMS). As noted earlier, these systems operate in tandem with a network of sensors located throughout the building and externally. The sensors monitor the environmental conditions and relay the information back to a computer which in turn controls all components of the building's airconditioning system.

Having been programmed with the desired set points, the computer can then make adjustments to the passage of air and other factors to ensure that these set points are achieved and, if they are not, to alert you that a problem has arisen.

Economy cycle

Modern airconditioning systems can today operate by what is known as an economy cycle. This means that the levels of air entering and leaving the building are controlled to achieve energy savings by not overworking the plant when external conditions closely match the desired internal conditions.

The following table shows some of the most commonly used airconditioning acronyms which you will often see on plans and drawings, as well as pipes and other equipment in your plant room.

Power and Lighting

Purpose-built repositories can consume large amounts of energy and lighting is one of the major contributors to this. A building with an overall floor area comprising many thousands of square metres will require considerable quantities of light fittings, and their operation and replacement can be both costly and time consuming.[16]

Atria and other large expanses of glass, such as light wells and skylights, are attractive and aesthetically pleasing. They certainly have their usefulness in allowing the passage of natural light, but they should be limited to foyers and general public or office areas. However, given the transfer capabilities of glass it needs to be heavily filtered in order to control both heat migration and the passage of ultraviolet light.

The National Archives of Canada's Gatineau facility has a very large glass atrium. It is visually quite striking and pleasing but may in time lead to difficulties maintaining stable environmental conditions in the area and contribute to high energy costs.

GLOSSARY OF AIRCONDITIONING ACRONYMS

AHU	air handling unit
BMS	building management system
CHW	chilled water
CHWV	chilled water valve
dC	degrees Celsius
dF	degrees Fahrenheit
EWT	entering water temperature
HVAC	heating, ventilation, airconditioning
HWV	hot water valve
LWT	leaving water temperature
OA	outside air
OAHU	outside airhandling unit
RA	return air
RAF	return air fan
RARH	return air relative humidity
RAT	return air temperature
RH	relative humidity
SA	supply air
SAF	supply air fan
SARH	supply air relative humidity
SAT	supply air temperature

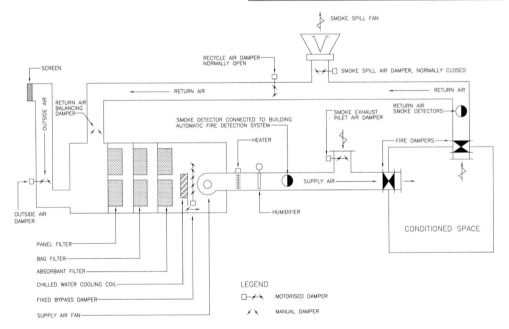

A typical airconditioning system.
Drawing by John de Salis of the National Archives of Australia.

Lighting and energy management

In recent times, energy management has assumed great prominence, so much so that many government agencies are required to include references to this subject as part of their annual reports. Given that purpose-built repositories have airconditioning plants operating 24 hours a day and have large expanses of lighting, containing energy usage has proven to be a daunting task. Nevertheless, there have been a number of recent innovations which have arisen as a direct response to the challenge, ie the use of controlled lighting in storage areas, assessment of tariffs available from electricity suppliers and the detailed monitoring of energy accounts.

Many institutions have had time switches connected to their light fittings, both to save electricity costs and to reduce the amount of light in the storage areas. Such devices can be controlled through a building management system. If your staff forget to turn off the lights, the timer will automatically disconnect at a predetermined interval, say 15 minutes. Provision should also be made to override the timed switch if lighting is required for lengthy periods.

You should ensure that lighting brightness is appropriate for each area of your building. Brightness is measured in lux levels. In highly used staffing and public areas levels should range from 240–400 lux. The levels in storage areas should be lower and set between 80–240 lux, depending on the rate of usage in those areas.[17]

It is also important to note that overhead lighting in the storage areas should run perpendicular to the shelving and not in the same direction. In this way, lighting will be available no matter where a person happens to be inside each row of shelving. If lighting runs in the same direction as the shelving there can be numerous 'blind spots'.

Lighting controls for storage areas should be separate to the remainder of the building and each area should be divided into separate lighting zones. A person should not have to light up an entire floor or storage area if they simply require access to a small area only.

An interesting innovation in this regard is the use of motion detectors and infra-red beams to control the lighting in storage areas at the Queensland State Archives' Runcorn facility. Sensors are strategically placed so that if a person enters an area, motion detectors will activate the lighting in the main corridors. Entering a row of mobile shelving breaks the beam and this too activates the lighting directly above that row. The lights remain on for a set period (although this period is adjustable). This system can be a boon for staff loaded with boxes or other items. A manual override system ensures that lighting is available for longer periods if needed. Again, timers can switch off the lights if staff forget to do it.[18]

You should make careful note of the local electricity supplier's tariffs and be careful when commencing operations each day that all major users of power do not start at once. If the airconditioning plant for the office areas and all lighting units are switched on together, the resulting power spike could result in higher energy charges. It is desirable that such services be introduced gradually, say over an hour or so. A building management system can undertake this task effortlessly.

Energy management has also led to changes in the design of facilities, modifications being made which help to ensure that conditions within a building – once established – can readily be sustained. These changes, some of which have already been mentioned, have included more efficient use of airconditioning systems and a more effective use of insulation in the ceilings and walls of the storage areas.

Once again, the need for a fully sealed internal environment assumes prominence. You should ensure there are no gaps around doors, windows and their frames. If there are such gaps they should be repaired quickly. Otherwise all you are doing is paying high energy costs to maintain environmental conditions which are simply not being achieved.

Emergency power supplies

Depending on the formats and value of the records held, you may need to consider the inclusion of an emergency generator to ensure uninterrupted power in the event of a failure in the mains supply. Many modern facilities – including East Burwood, Runcorn and Kwun Tong – have emergency power units. In reality, they are only necessary if power outages are likely to exceed 48 hours.

Generators, which are usually diesel powered, can ensure that the airconditioning system remains operable and that other essential services, such as lighting and computers, are available. They can be supplied in many capacities. It is essential that, if a decision is made to install a generator, correct loads are calculated beforehand. The total power needed to operate your airconditioning plant, lighting, fire and security systems and computers should be ascertained and it should be ensured that the generator can provide this power, preferably with some reserve.

Protection against power surges, as opposed to complete power failures, can be provided in the form of an uninterrupted power supply unit (UPS). The unit will help smooth or flatten erratic power supplies and ensure that the voltage remains at the right level. This is turn will protect delicate equipment such as computers. Additionally, smaller surge guards can be attached to the power outlets providing protection for individual computers.

Case Study Number 3 – *The National Archives´ Villawood Repository – Environmental Conditions and Energy Management*

The problem

The National Archives' Villawood repository was built in the 1970s, though its design was even older. It had large, open plan storage areas of more than 3 000 square metres. There were no airlocks to the storage areas, the spaces were poorly sealed with gaps around the door frames and, in some cases, around airconditioning vents. There were windows in most storage areas.

In addition, airconditioning controls were obsolete and not energy efficient in their operation. There had been many changes over the years and the drawings and documentation were no longer adequate.

There were large expanses of overhead lighting with limited control. Generally, it was the case that all lighting was activated at the one time, even if access was only required to one part of the area.

These factors meant that it was difficult to maintain strict environmental controls and energy costs were extremely high. By the early 1990s, it was recognised that substantial changes needed to be made.

The solution

A program involving a number of steps was developed to overcome the problems. Some of these steps were expensive, but necessary.

The large, open plan storage areas remain (though they would not be repeated in future buildings), but airlocks were installed. All gaps around windows and door frames and other items were sealed. All windows exposed to direct sunlight were covered, insulated and enclosed with wood panelling.

A completely new building management system involving direct digital controls was installed. In addition, all defective wiring and some defective components were replaced, eg some motors which operated the dampers had long ago burnt out. In fact, a whole new control philosophy was designed for the building's HVAC (heating, ventilation and airconditioning) system by utilising recent advancements in electronic controls and coupling these with the building management system.

The lighting for the storage areas was rewired into zones so that not all lighting was required for a particular storage area. Time switches were installed so that the lighting would switch off at predetermined intervals. Manual override switches were included so that staff who needed to remain in an area for a long period would not have to continually reset the system.

A detailed assessment of the local energy supplier's tariffs was made and measures were developed to utilise these tariffs more efficiently, eg not having all equipment, such as airconditioning components and lighting, start at once with each new working day.

Greater recognition was given to the efficient use of airconditioning plant, particularly when external conditions closely matched the desired internal conditions. Such actions reduced wear and tear on the plant and helped to lower energy costs.

The results

Environmental controls for the storage areas are regularly maintained and energy costs have been substantially reduced.

In the circumstances as described above, the solutions were tailored to Villawood's design. Not all of these measures would work in all storage facilities. Each has to be assessed on its merits. As a general point, it can be stated with certainty that maintaining a sealed environment and efficient use of plant and equipment, as well as understanding and utilising energy supplier's tariffs, will go a long way towards the maintenance of appropriate environmental conditions and reduced energy costs.

Lessons learned

The lessons that were learned from the Villawood experience include:

- the avoidance of large open, plan storage areas;
- the need for the maintenance of fully sealed storage areas;
- the need for accurate airconditioning controls;
- an appreciation of greater use of external environmental conditions when they approximate the desired internal conditions;
- the need of regular studies of energy suppliers' tariffs and appropriate actions to utilise these tariffs;
- the maintenance of accurate drawings and documentation of all work undertaken; and
- the need for zoned lighting and time switches.

Fire Safety

Given the valuable and often irreplaceable nature of the records held within a repository, it is obvious that fire protection is paramount.[19]

While building codes and legislation vary across the Australian States and Territories, and from one country to another, this section describes what are considered to be the minimum requirements for a modern purpose-built repository. As with so many other features of repository management, they have evolved progressively over the years. You should seek specialist advice during the building's design phase, from both the architect and fire safety experts.

The most important measure with respect to fire safety is of course prevention. Good housekeeping, training of staff and ensuring that all safety systems are appropriately maintained will go a long way towards protecting you from the ravages of fire.

Reactive measures can broadly be divided into two categories – detection and suppression. There are a number of factors that apply to each. The primary intention of these measures is to detect the fire at the earliest opportunity, ensure the speedy removal of all people within the building and then extinguish the fire as quickly as possible.

Fire detection and people safety

First, your building should have a central alarm panel, sometimes referred to as a fire indicator panel (FIP). The panel should have a direct connection to the local fire brigade or monitoring service which ensures that in the event of an alarm the brigade is notified automatically. A series of smoke and heat detectors should be located at appropriate points throughout the building, each connected to the central panel.[20]

In confined spaces, such as computer centres, audiovisual vaults and security vaults, you should also consider the installation of an early warning smoke detection system. There are several products available today, including *VESDA*™ (Very Early Smoke Detection Apparatus). They are highly sensitive, designed to sense the presence of smoke before a fire has fully developed.

One word of warning – if extensive cleaning of a storage area is planned, the early warning smoke detection system should be switched off. Their sensitivity means they are likely to be activated by swirling dust particles.

In those buildings where evacuation of people may be a complicated task, possibly due to the large size of the building or its extensive compartmentalisation, consideration may be given to an emergency warning and intercommunication system (EWIS). The system enables fire wardens to communicate with each other, and the fire brigade, to brief staff during an emergency and to allow the staged evacuation of a facility.

Your building should have exits at appropriate locations. Illuminated emergency and exit lighting should be installed indicating the way to these exits. You should remember that in the storage areas, where there are large expanses of high mobile shelving, you may need several signs to assist people in quickly locating the exits.

Fire containment and suppression

In addition to rapidly detecting a fire, there needs to be the means for containing it and then quickly extinguishing it. Obviously a major conflagration could never be tackled by staff, yet the means should exist for preventing such a scenario from developing in the first place.

The facility must, of course, have reliable access to a regular water supply. In this respect, advances in modern technology have actually helped to reduce overall construction costs. The design of the National Archives' Villawood repository included provision for underground water storage tanks with a capacity of 450 000 litres. The theory was that in the event of a fire and the loss of mains pressure, the tanks could be brought into service with the aid of pumps. Nowadays, this is recognised as both costly and excessive and a simpler alternative can be the use of multiple connections to the main water supply.

The use of smaller storage compartments rather than large, open plan floor spaces – as described in chapter 2 – will assist with fire protection. Dividing a building into compartments not only aids the maintenance of a conditioned environment, it helps to control the spread of flames and smoke.

Each compartment should be linked by means of fire doors which, in turn, are connected to the central fire alarm panel. The doors are held in the open position by means of magnetic seals, controlled by the central panel. When an alarm is activated, the seals are broken and the doors close automatically.

Again, as stated in chapter 2, all walls and doors surrounding the storage areas should be fire rated, with a two hour period suggested as the minimum rating and four hours if sprinklers or other forms of extinguishment are not used.

Modern research has shown that, in the event of a fire, the real risk to people is the smoke, not the flames. The task, therefore, is to contain the spread of smoke and ensure its swift removal from the building. There are two ways this can be achieved if the building has not been compartmentalised. First, smoke curtains can be installed. These are basically barriers made from galvanised steel sheeting which extend part way down from the ceiling. They are designed to trap the smoke within a given space and stop it from spreading across the entire storage area.

Complementing the curtains is a smoke exhaust system. The system will be activated in the event of an emergency and pump the smoke out of the building, either through outlets in the roof or the walls.

The building's airconditioning system should be connected to the central alarm panel so that in an emergency the system either shuts down automatically or the smoke exhaust system comes into operation. Dampers in the airconditioning ducting also assist this process. Basically, they are barriers which drop or lock into place, sealing the ducts and preventing the spread of smoke through the entire system.

Internal fire hose reels and hand held extinguishers should be installed at appropriate points. Hand held extinguishers should be located near major exits or exit routes.

Last, it is strongly recommended that a fire suppressant system be installed in all storage areas. Generally, this can take the form of a sprinkler system, using water or foam, or a gas flood system. Whatever system is installed, it should be connected to the central alarm panel.

Sprinkler systems

There are a number of different types of sprinkler systems available today. The most common, however, are wet pipe, dry pipe, on-off, foam and misting.[21]

Wet pipe

This system is widely used and incorporates water as the suppressant. An array of sprinkler heads are attached to the ceilings or walls, each head having a fusible link or frangible (breakable) bulb. In the event of a fire, the link melts or the bulb breaks and the water is released. It should be noted that only those heads affected by the fire will activate; the remainder should not.

Dry pipe

Despite the name, this system uses water too, but on a delayed basis. The piping is filled with compressed air which is released when a sprinkler head is activated. The water follows shortly after. The system is generally only used in areas where freezing of the water in the piping may be a cause for concern. Again, only those heads affected by the fire will activate; the remainder should not.

On-Off

The system uses water, but once the fire has been extinguished, and the temperature drops below a predetermined level, the heads switch off automatically. Should the fire be rekindled, the system will reactivate. Again, only those heads affected by the fire will activate; the remainder should not. It should be noted that this type of system is more expensive than the conventional wet pipe system.

Foam

In these systems, the suppressant is not water but expansion foam which replaces oxygen and smothers the fire.

Misting

Misting is a variation of the sprinkler system, using water in a very fine mist form, the water being forced out under pressure. In this way, the volume of water is considerably less than would be used for a conventional wet pipe system. The fine droplets not only draw the heat from the fire, they also turn to steam which covers the fire and thus excludes the oxygen.[22]

Using sprinkler systems

The use of sprinklers in archival repositories, particularly wet pipe, is a controversial issue and does not have universal acceptance. Some institutions prefer not to have them, placing their trust in a quick response from the fire brigade.

Generally, sprinklers are not a requirement of law or Australian Standard, though this is in some cases dependent on the size of the building or its proximity to other buildings. Neither are they a requirement of British Standard (BS) 5454 or DIS 11799: 1998.[23] They are, however, recommended in the National Fire Protection Association's *Manual for Fire Protection for Archives and Records Centers*.[24] Further, Irena G Shepilova and Adrienne G Thomas suggest they should be 'mandatory', particularly for those archives and libraries using mobile shelving,[25] which, of course, most would.

Despite the lack of total acceptance, many institutions have adhered to the principle of using sprinkler, or similar, systems. The National Archives is one of these institutions and, irrespective of whether a building is owned or leased, and irrespective of the value of the records to be stored, the Archives will not use a building that does not have sprinklers.

Apart from the installation costs, one of the major objections to sprinkler systems is the fear of accidental discharge, eg the mythical workman with a ladder who accidentally breaks one of the sprinkler heads and causes flooding as a result. In more than 30 years, the National Archives has had only one mishap with sprinklers and that involved a faulty pipe, not a sprinkler head.

While there is the possibility of accidental leakage, the chances of this occurring are remote for several reasons. First, sprinkler heads can be covered with small metal guards to protect them against breakage. Second, you should be aware that sprinkler heads operate independently, so that if a fire is detected, or an accident does occur, only a small number of heads will be activated, not the entire system. The only way the entire system would operate is if the building was subject to a major conflagration.

A second objection to the use of sprinklers is the possibility that over time the pipes may rust and begin to leak. To help counteract this possibility, you should ensure that the pipes in your system are made from high quality material, such as stainless steel.

If the water from sprinklers is a cause for concern, the volume of water from the fire brigade's hoses, and the velocity with which this water is ejected, is far worse. You only have to read the 1995 report of the fire which affected the Norfolk Record Office, England, to appreciate the damage that can be caused by the brigade in putting out a fire.[26]

Finally, there is one simple home truth that should never be overlooked – wet records are easier to retrieve and repair than burnt ones.

Gas flood systems

In the past, gas flood systems have been used in small, confined storage areas such as security vaults, or where the physical nature of the records would be adversely affected by water, eg film storage vaults. Today, however, gas flood systems are commonly found in larger storage areas too.

Carbon Dioxide

At one stage, the most commonly used gas was carbon dioxide and, in some circumstances, it is still in use today. It is a good fire extinguishant as it displaces oxygen but, on the negative side, it is life threatening to any persons who may be trapped in the area being protected.

Halon

Halon evolved as an alternative to carbon dioxide. It had the advantage of being a fire extinguishant that was not as life threatening.

The gas was produced in two forms. The first – bromotrifluoromethane (BTM) or halon 1301 – was used in flood systems for vaults and store rooms; the gas being housed in large yellow cylinders. The second type – bromochlorodifluoromethane (BCF) or halon 1211 – was found in hand held extinguishers and was used for electrical fires and flammable materials. Again, the extinguishers were easily recognised by their yellow colour.

For a number of years, halon was widely used by archival institutions, libraries and museums throughout the world. Unfortunately, the gas is a chloro-fluorocarbon (or CFC) and in recent years CFCs have been shown to damage the ozone layer. Since the early 1990s halon has been phased out of most archival facilities worldwide, in line with the Montreal Protocol of 1987. In Australia, unless an institution had been granted 'essential use' status (and this would not normally apply to an archives) stocks of halon had to be withdrawn from service by 1 January 1996.[27]

TABLE 5 FIRE SUPPRESSANT SYSTEMS CURRENTLY IN USE

Facility	Institution	Fire Suppressant
Villawood	National Archives	Wet pipe sprinkler system
East Burwood	National Archives	Wet pipe sprinkler system
Kingswood	Archives Office of New South Wales	None in early stages; wet pipe in later stages
Runcorn	Queensland State Archives	Wet pipe sprinkler system
Berriedale	Archives Office of Tasmania	None
Portside	BHP Pty Ltd	Wet pipe sprinkler system
Wellington	National Archives of New Zealand	Wet pipe sprinkler system
Nouville	Archives Territoriales, New Caldeonia	None
College Park	National Archives and Records Administration, USA	Wet pipe sprinkler system
Gatineau	National Archives of Canada	Dry pipe sprinkler system
Kew	Public Record Office, UK	None
Koblenz	Bundesarchiv, Germany	Dry pipe sprinkler system
Arningedepan	Riksarkivet, Sweden	None
Ulleval Hageby	Riksarkivet, National Archives of Norway	None
Beijing	Beijing Municipal Archives	Gas - halon 1301 (due for replacement)
Shanghai	Shanghai Municipal Archives	Gas - alkyl halide
Kwun Tong	Public Records Office, Hong Kong	Gas - FM200
Taejon	Government Archives and Records Service, Republic of Korea	Gas - NAFS III
Canning Rise	National Archives of Singapore	Dry pipe sprinkler system

New generation gases

With the demise of halon, there has been considerable research worldwide to find a suitable alternative. As an interim measure, the most appropriate strategy has been to use a combination of wet pipe sprinklers and an early warning smoke detection system. This combination has been used in a number of locations, including East Burwood, Runcorn and Portside.

Today's stricter environmental controls mean that new gases must have zero ozone depleting potential (ODP) and their global warming potential (GWP) must also be taken into account. Furthermore, it would be ideal if they have the potential to simply be connected directly to the former halon discharge system. This 'drop in' potential of new gases would negate the need for costly new pipework and additional control installations.

Several new gases have already been developed and marketed. They include:

- *Inergen*™, a German product, consisting of nitrogen, argon and carbon dioxide;
- *FM200*™, developed by the American company Firemaster; and
- *NAFS III*™, also an American development (this gas has a low ozone depletion potential and as such is referred to as a 'transitional product', meaning that it can only be used until 2015, by which time it too will need replacement).[28]

In time, more gases will no doubt appear. The novelty of these gases means that they have been used in relatively few locations and at this stage it is not possible to comment on their effectiveness as fire suppressants.

Regardless of which system you decide to adopt – whether sprinklers or gas – there are two noteworthy points. The obvious point is that you should have a fire suppressant and, second, you should consult with fire safety experts in order to ascertain which system is the most appropriate for your facility.

Table 5 illustrates the types of fire suppressant systems that have been incorporated in a number of facilities worldwide.

College Park uses a wet pipe sprinkler system but has adopted a most interesting strategy as part of its fire protection program. In the event of an alarm, all shelving units automatically open about 200 millimetres so that if the sprinklers are activated, water will be able to reach inside the shelving, putting the fire out faster than might otherwise be the case. The gaps created by this action also act as a 'flue' and should prevent the fire travelling across shelving units.[29] However, as College Park uses electrically operated shelving it is an easy task to do this; most institutions which use manually operated shelving would not be able to accomplish this feat.

Fire surveys

In addition to fire detection and suppression, it is suggested that you should undertake a formal fire survey at regular intervals to ensure that your facility maintains its fire protection capability. The survey should preferably be conducted by a fire safety expert. With the passage of time, advancements in technology and building codes, it can easily transpire that a facility which once fully met all fire safety requirements no longer does. It may be that your emergency procedures are inadequate or non-existent. Or it may be that housekeeping practices have been allowed to degenerate or emergency exits have been blocked by stores. These are some of the matters the expert should be asked to report on. The Commonwealth Fire Board recommends that surveys be held every 3 years.[30]

Earlier, reference was made to the importance of fire prevention. In this context, you should never regard fire surveys solely as the province of experts and simply wait for them to be done every 3 years. There are a number of basic checks that form part of good housekeeping and can be undertaken by anyone on a regular basis. Such checks can include an inspection of exits to ensure they are not blocked, verification that fire extinguishers are in position and clearly marked, and that combustible materials remain in low quantities.[31] By following a simple program such as this, you may help prevent a fire from ever starting and that really is what it is all about.

Education and training

Last, the most basic point of all. All staff should be educated and trained in fire safety. There is little point in having expensive equipment, such as an EWIS system, or hand held extinguishers located strategically throughout the building, if the staff do not know where they are or how to use them, or what to do in the event of an emergency.

Emergency procedures should be prepared and everyone should have a copy. All staff should know where the exits are and where to meet after they have left the building. To ensure that this happens, fire drills should be conducted on a regular basis.

Security

The level of security afforded to a purpose-built repository is often considered solely in terms of the sensitivity of records held or their potential value to unauthorised users. But security needs to be contemplated in a broader context. In addition to protecting your record collection, there is the need to protect staff and visitors, assets within the building (such as computers) and last, the building itself.[32]

At the outset, it can be stated that the most common form of security risk will probably involve vandalism or actions by disgruntled former employees.

FIRE SAFETY CHECKLIST
Central alarm panel
Smoke/heat detectors
Early warning smoke detection system (eg VESDA™)
Emergency warning and intercommunication system (EWIS)
Emergency exits and illuminated lighting
Adequate water supply
Fire doors
Fire rated walls and doors
Smoke curtains (if large, open plan areas are used)
Smoke exhaust system
Hose reels
Hand held extinguishers
Fire suppression system (sprinklers, foam or gas)
Fire surveys every three years
Staff training and education
Emergency procedures

Securing the building

Your building should have a central alarm panel which, in turn, is connected to a monitoring point. This latter point will either be an external security company, or it may be an internal centre if your institution is large enough to bear the cost of such a centre. Technology has reached the stage where all forms of access to a building and within the building, whether authorised or unauthorised, can now be detected through a variety of devices each of which is directly connected to the central panel.

Typically, all of the building's external perimeter openings (including doors, windows, loading bay doors and plant room doors) should be fitted with reed switches connected to the panel. Such switches create a seal which, when broken, registers as an alarm on the panel. Motion detectors can also be placed at strategic intervals throughout the building and can especially be used to cover points of entry to storage areas. Again, they are connected to the central panel.

It may also be considered necessary to install cameras in public areas, including foyers and reading rooms, with monitors located in staffing areas, or at a central monitoring point. Video recorders can be connected to the monitors to provide a record of all that has been observed.

When designing public areas (and this will be covered in more detail in chapter 4) you should remember that pillars can hide activities that people may not want seen and it is preferable that their use in reading rooms be avoided if possible. If they are there, then cameras or mirrors may be needed to monitor the blind spots they cause.

Entrance doors to storage areas should be locked and only appropriate staff should have access to these areas. Access can be controlled through traditional keying or there are a wide variety of electric or electronic access systems available, eg cypher locks, swipe cards, proximity cards or key cards.

At this point, remember that your building will be accessed not only by staff and readers, but other members of the public as well, eg maintenance contractors and cleaners. Their movement through the building, and particularly the storage areas, should also be monitored.

Securing the site

In addition to the building, the security of the surrounding grounds should also be considered. The inclusion of a perimeter security fence generally acts as a deterrent to vandals and those intruders seeking an easy target for petty theft. In this context, the National Archives' Darwin facility suffered from vandalism on a number of occasions until a secure fence was erected around the perimeter of the site. Similarly, the Archives' Rosny Park (Hobart, Tasmania) facility experienced a number of attacks of petty vandalism until a fence was installed.

Consideration may also be given to random patrols of the site in the silent hours by a security company unless there is a guard or caretaker in residence.

As your institution has a duty of care for your staff, and visitors too, it is desirable that lighting be installed throughout the grounds, particularly if your building sits on a large site. It is especially important that the carparks be well lit at night to ensure the safety of persons using the building. Any areas where an assailant might hide, eg behind large bushes or shrubs should be noted and remedial action taken.

Security surveys

As with fire surveys, a formal security survey should be undertaken at regular intervals. The National Archives schedules surveys for each of its facilities every five years. The survey should be undertaken by a security expert who should ensure that the building has maintained its security levels and, where appropriate, continues to meet relevant building codes and legislation. The survey should also include a threat evaluation.

A threat evaluation is where a judgement is made about the likelihood or probability of an event taking place that could adversely affect your resources. It is used to determine if there is a threat, and, if so, where that threat is likely to come from and how it might be realised.

Threats can be accidental, eg fire, flood, equipment failure or negligence. They can also be deliberate, eg theft, sabotage, unauthorised disclosure or disruption to operations. Threats can emanate from dishonest or disgruntled employees or members of the public, criminals or terrorists.

If the following three factors, ie intention, capability and opportunity, are present and operating together, then a deliberate threat may actually happen. Any assessment of deliberate threats should examine the intention and capability of individuals or groups to cause harm to you. The opportunity for such harm then depends on the reliability and efficiency of your existing protective security arrangements and measures.

Education and training

Finally, it is a very basic point but one strongly worth noting. Most of today's security devices are 'hi-tech' and, in some cases, quite expensive. Yet your building's security is also completely dependent on something less elaborate and much less expensive, ie the cooperation of all staff and visitors. Without this cooperation, all the security measures you may have employed will be next to worthless.

If staff exit via a back door to have a cigarette and leave the door open, then your security has been violated. If staff leave their keys or access cards in a place where they might be stolen, then again, security can be violated. Likewise, if they notice someone in an area where they are not supposed to be and fail to seek confirmation of who that person is and why they are there.

All staff should be trained to appreciate the importance of security and the role they have to play in this regard. They should clearly understand that security should never be taken lightly.

SECURITY CHECKLIST

Security panel connected to a central monitoring point

Reed switches on all external building openings (doors and windows)

Motion detectors

Cameras and monitors

Controlled access into storage areas (locks)

Perimeter fencing

External lighting

Patrols of the site in the silent hours

Security surveys every five years

Staff training and education

---

1   Such literature includes: Tim Padfield, 'Climate control in libraries and archives', paper given to the Preservation of Library Materials Proceedings Conference held at the National Library of Vienna, April 1986, New York, 1987, volume 2, pp. 124–138; Guy Petherbridge, 'Environmental and housing considerations for the preservation of modern records – a guide for the records manager', *Proceedings of the 8th National Convention of the Records Management Association of Australia*, Darwin, 1991, pp. 122–173; Arnold den Teuling, 'Environmental conditions for the storage of archival materials', *Janus*, 1996.2, pp. 110–118; and William K Wilson, *Environmental guidelines for the storage of paper records: a technical report sponsored by the National Information Standards Organisation* (USA), NISO-TR01-1995, Bethesda, USA, 1995.

2   Guy Petherbridge, *Proceedings of the 8th National Convention of the Records Management Association of Australia*, pp. 136–141 and Archives Advice 1, *Protecting and Handling Paper Files*, National Archives 1997.

3   Guy Petherbridge, *Proceedings of the 8th National Convention of the Records Management Association of Australia*, pp. 148–156 and Archives Advice 7, *Protecting and Handling Photographs*, National Archives 1997.

4   Guy Petherbridge, *Proceedings of the 8th National Convention of the Records Management Association of Australia*, pp. 167–168 and Archives Advice 5, *Protecting and Handling Magnetic Media*, National Archives 1997.

5   Michel Duchein, *Archive Buildings and Equipment*, Munich, 1988, p. 105.

6   Arnold den Teuling, *Janus*, 1996.2, p. 111.

7   William K Wilson, *Environmental guidelines for the storage of paper records: a technical report sponsored by the National Information Standards Organisation* (USA), p. 2.

8   British Standard (BS) 5454, *Recommendations for Storage and Exhibition of Archival Documents*, London, 1989, p. 6.

9   ISO/TC46/SC10, Information and Documentation/Physical keeping of Documents – DIS 11799: 1998, *Information and Documentation - Storage Requirements for Archive and Library Materials*, Copenhagen, 1998, p. 13.

10 National Archives, *Guidelines for Environmental Conditions and Safety and Protection Levels for Storage*, Charts 1 and 2, Canberra, 1997.

11 James Druzik and Paul Banks, 'Appropriate standards for the indoor environment', *Conservation Administration News*, 62/63, 1995, pp. 2–9.

12 Parliamentary Standing Committee on Public Works, *Report relating to the proposed construction of an Archives Repository at Villawood, New South Wales*, Canberra, 1970, p. 13.

13 DIS 11799: 1998, Archives Advice 7, National Archives p. 4.

14 The lack of study on micro environmental conditions has been noted by David Thomas, 'Archive buildings: international comparisons', *Journal of the Society of Archivists*, vol. 9, no. 1, 1988, p. 44 and Petherbridge, *Proceedings of the 8th National Convention of the Records Management Association of Australia*, p. 133.

15 The following sources were used in preparing the description of an airconditioning system: Craig Stevens, *Airconditioning in National Archives*, Sydney, 1996; Carrier Corporation, *Basic Concepts of Airconditioning Systems*, New York, 1982; Carrier Corporation, *Central Station Air handling Equipment*, New York, 1984.

16 The section on power and lighting was prepared with the assistance of internal working documents, specifications and notes prepared by the National Archives´ Facilities Program.

17 Australian Standard 1680.1-1990 *Interior Lighting Part 1: General Principles and Recommendations*, Sydney, 1990, p. 16.

18 Vicki Warden, 'The New Queensland State Archives building', paper presented to the Conference of the Australian Society of Archivists, Townsville, 1994, p. 53.

19 The section on fire safety was prepared with the assistance of internal working documents, specifications and notes prepared by the National Archives´ Facilities Program and consultation with Mr Brian Hay, Senior Officer (Technical) with the Secretariat of the Commonwealth Fire Board, Melbourne.

20 The number and placement of smoke and heat detectors is spelt out in various Australian Standards but fire safety experts should of course be consulted in this regard.

21 Information regarding sprinkler systems has been taken from Standards Australia, *Automatic Fire Sprinkler Systems*, 2118.1-1995, Sydney, 1995, pp. 13–18 and National Fire Protection Association, *Manual for Fire Protection for Archives and Records Centers*, NFPA 232AM, Quincy, 1986, pp. 9–10.

22 Further information on misting systems will be found in a number of sources including: Commonwealth Fire Board Fire Safety Circular 91, pp. 4–5; Roger S McKay, 'Fine Water Spray – A Halon Replacement Option', *Fire Surveyor*, June 1993, pp. 16–20; and David P Smith, 'Water Mist Fire Suppression', *Fire Safety Engineering*, vol. 2, no. 2, 1995, pp. 10–15.

23 British Standard (BS) 5454 (page 5) states that a repository should have an automatic fire-extinguishing system but does not specify what this system should be. DIS 11799: 1998 recommends that a fire extinguishing system be considered, whether water or gas, but does not insist that this be done.

24 Irena G Shepilova and Adrienne G Thomas, *Main Principles of Fire Protection in Libraries and Archives: A RAMP study*, Paris, 1992, p. 16.

25 National Fire Protection Association, *Manual for Fire Protection for Archives and Records Centers*, pp. 9, 14.

26 Jean Kennedy, 'Norfolk Record Office fire: an initial report', *Journal of the Society of Archivists*, vol. 16, no. 1, 1995, pp. 3–6.

27 Commonwealth Fire Board Fire Safety Circular 91, *Halon Fire Extinguishants: Alternative Fire Protection Strategies*, 1994, p. 1.

28 Commonwealth Fire Board Fire Safety Circular 91, pp. 3–4.

29 Michele F Pacifico, 'The National Archives at College Park', *Government Information Quarterly*, vol. 13, no. 2, 1996, p. 122.

30 Commonwealth Fire Board Fire Safety Circular 80, *Fire Safety Surveys*, 1993, p. 2.

31 Commonwealth Fire Board Fire Safety Circular 74, *Fire Safety Checks by Occupants*, 1992, provides a list of basic checks that can be undertaken by anyone at any time.

32 The section on security was prepared with the assistance of internal working documents and security survey notes prepared by the National Archives´ Facilities Program.

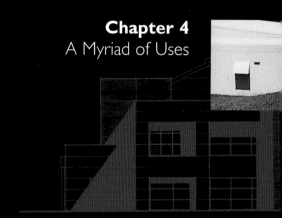

Chapter 4
A Myriad of Uses

EAST

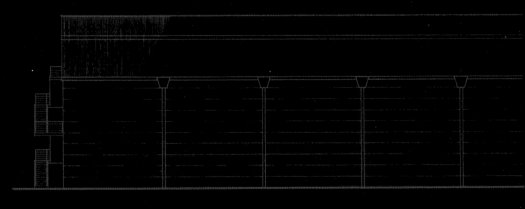

SOUTH

Because records are created in many physical formats, you will require just as many means of storing, protecting and accessing them.

The records will be consulted by the agencies that created them, the public and staff. No doubt some records will require conservation treatment as well. Your new building must cater for all of these uses.

Special Purpose Storage Areas

Considered here are smaller, special purpose storage areas, as opposed to large expanses of open storage.[1]

Large objects storage area

Storage areas may need to be specifically designed to house records such as models, objects and other material of irregular size which cannot be catered for in standard shelving. Such items can generally be held in a dedicated area supplied with racking.

If your institution has large holdings of plans, drawings or posters, you may need to provide an area for their storage, either in plan cabinets or fixed or mobile racking. The aisleways around shelving installations such as these should be sufficient to allow the movement of staff pushing trolleys or carrying the objects.

The respository area of the National Archives' office in Canberra under construction. This room will be used to hold the records most heavily used at the office.
Photograph by Barry Brown.

Low temperature/controlled atmosphere storage area

If you have a collection of audiovisual material or magnetic media, you will need a secure storage facility to ensure the maintenance of environmental parameters which in this case are quite critical.

Strict airconditioning controls and good filtration are especially important. The area should, of course, be completely sealed. The walls, floor and the ceiling should be resistant to the passage of moisture, and this usually is provided by means of vapour barriers. In order to further ensure the maintenance of conditions, and to prevent the entry of dust and other contaminants, airlocks – and possibly wind curtains – can also be provided.

It may also be desirable to install an acclimatisation room. The room is used to acclimatise records as they are being transferred into, or out of, the designated storage area. In many cases, transferring an item without acclimatisation can lead to the development of condensation and cause damage to the item.

Security vault storage

A secure storage area may be needed if your institution holds classified records or records that may be culturally sensitive or financially valuable.

Depending on the nature of the records, the area may require walls made of reinforced concrete and steel doors with combination locks. Security measures may even extend to installing intruder proof grills in the airconditioning ducts servicing the area. Other devices, including alarms and video surveillance, will probably also be required.

Agency records examination area

Some institutions allow agencies to examine their own records on site if, for example, they are appraising and sentencing the records stored on their behalf. If this is the case, a designated area will need to be provided.

Such areas are generally fairly basic, usually only containing a small amount of storage and some desk space. A large sorting table is also useful.

Records transit area

An area will need to be set aside to allow the processing of records as they enter and leave the building, or if they need to be relocated within the building. Such an area is, of course, best located near the loading dock.

The room will require the inclusion of static or mobile shelving to house the records while they await pick up or return. Staff working in the area will require benches or desktops.

Even though the records are housed in this area on a temporary basis, the nature of the records means that the area should be airconditioned and the lighting should be filtered to guard against the damage caused by ultraviolet light, or alternatively low output ultraviolet lights should be installed.

Sorting area

From time to time, records in a large repository will require sorting, listing, repackaging or reboxing. So, an area needs to be set aside to enable staff to undertake this work.

The room will require a small amount of static or mobile shelving for temporary storage purposes. The staff will require desktops, benches or tables so they can spread the records out prior to sorting and reboxing.

Again, the nature of the records means that airconditioning and lighting should be of the same standard as would apply to the permanent storage areas.

Box store

A box store will normally be needed to house the containers that are to be supplied to clients or to enable the reboxing of records held within the facility. It should be located near the loading dock.

Boxes are normally supplied in large bundles which are heavy and bulky to move so the walls of the box store should be solid, or at least braced, to protect them against damage when the boxes are being moved.

It is also desirable that double doors be used for the entrance to the store to enable the movement of bundles into and out of the area. The doors should also be provided with metal cladding as they will be subject to a fair amount of abuse. The door height should be sufficient to allow forklift access if necessary.

Conservation Laboratories

A conservation laboratory can have many functions – an area for cleaning, deacidification, repair, encapsulation and copying.[2] These activities can apply to records in a wide array of physical formats – such as paper, textiles, films, magnetic tapes, models and leather bound books.[3]

The layout of a typical conservation laboratory is therefore dependent on the physical nature of the records being held and the activities that are likely to be undertaken. Today, not all conservation functions are undertaken in-house; many are contracted out.

Providing for conservation can be quite an elaborate undertaking. The National Archives of Canada's Gatineau

A conservator cleaning and repacking negatives in the dry area at the National Archives of Australia's facility in Mitchell, Canberra.

facilities have been likened to a 'conservation village'; an area of 4 500 square metres and a staff of 60 conservators and 10 administrators.[4] The Queensland State Archives' Runcorn facility has eight separate conservation areas.[5] The National Archives of Singapore has provision for 10 conservators at its new Canning Rise facility.[6]

On the other hand, facilities can be virtually nil if the budget will not allow it or a decision has been made to contract the function to some other agency. What follows, therefore, is a generalised description of a typical laboratory.

At the outset, it is necessary to make a few basic points about designing a conservation laboratory. First, there is a need to be flexible, to use demountable partitioning as much as possible and other items such as mobile or 'stand alone' furniture and equipment. In short, anything that can readily be modified, added or removed at a later stage if necessary. This, of course, helps you to adapt to any future changes involving record formats or the way in which records themselves are treated.

Second, you should remember that, in addition to work facilities, it is necessary to provide for the comfort and safety of conservation staff.

Last, the area needs to be secure. Sometimes, in the process of performing conservation treatment, items are reduced to a particularly vulnerable state, so they need to be protected from inadvertent handling or damage. Likewise, conservation equipment itself may be dangerous if handled by untrained staff.

Laboratories should be well lit by a combination of natural and artificial light. If windows are to be included they should be tinted to filter direct sunlight and absorb ultraviolet radiation. It should not be forgotten that permanent value records will be temporarily located in these areas and they will generally be in a poor state of repair (otherwise they would not need conservation treatment).

Artificial light should be plentiful, but high efficiency ultraviolet filters should be fitted or low output ultraviolet lights should be installed. For work benches, lighting levels of 400 lux are recommended given the frequent use that will be made of these areas.[7]

The laboratory

This is the principal area where treatment takes place. It combines the activities of a traditional paper conservator and, possibly, conservation scientist, bookbinder and photographer. There will be a number of facilities required, including benches, sinks and fume cupboards as well as equipment for deacidification, bookbinding and encapsulation.[8]

Generally speaking, the typical laboratory can be divided into wet and dry work areas. The wet area covers such functions as humidification and deacidification. The dry area covers basic cleaning, document repair and encapsulation.

Wet area

One of the main factors contributing to the deterioration of paper is acidity. Acid, mainly sulphuric, breaks the links of cellulose polymer chains, reducing the strength of paper fibres. One way to combat acidity is to wash and deacidify documents. Therefore, a deacidification trough is recommended with plumbing on one side leaving three sides available for access.

By its very nature, deacidification requires large quantities of pure water, therefore a purifier should be connected to the plumbing but separate to that of the sink. An additional tap from the purifier to the sink will be necessary to ensure the water remains as pure as possible.

Sinks should be large enough to enable documents to fit inside them and there should be good quality heavy-duty taps designed to withstand high usage. Provision should be made for both hot and cold water supplies. As strong solvents are likely to be used in wet areas, stainless steel is the ideal material for all sinks, troughs and splashbacks.

As the floor may be subject to wetting from water and possibly chemical spillage, it is suggested that non-slip chemical resistant tiles be used. There should also be a waste outlet from the floor in case of major spillage or cleaning.

Most laboratories have a fume cupboard. If so, an exhaust fan should be installed to extract various gases. Wet areas must have a flammable liquid cabinet for the storage of chemicals which are used in the fume cabinets.

Dry area

Provision will need to be made for substantial bench space. The benches should be of such dimensions (height and depth) that will allow the conservators both the room and the ease of being able to work on large items such as plans.

Cupboards, drawers and shelves should be built into the benches, though there should also be sufficient knee spaces to allow staff sitting adjacent somewhere to put their legs. While this may seem obvious, more than one laboratory has been built without these knee spaces, preventing staff from sitting close to the benches.

It is also a good idea to have a supply of mobile tables that can be rearranged as modules in order to provide you with a smaller or larger work area as needed.

There should be a plentiful supply of power outlets. For this reason, it is suggested that consideration should be given to an overhead power supply system with sufficient outlets for benches and desks.

Airing room

A major conservation problem is the effect on records of mould, fungi and insect infestation, often as a result of a disaster such as flooding or possibly inadequate storage elsewhere. Records which demonstrate signs of this are quarantined in an airing room, away from other material, to avoid contamination until they can be treated and the problems resolved. The airing room should be designed as an open and uncluttered layout and be serviced by water and electricity.

The water supply is necessary to service a large stainless steel trough where records can be cleaned and for hosing down the floor to remove all traces of mould. The floor should, of course, be tiled and should have a drainage outlet.

An airing room needs fresh air and natural light for the treatment of mould. Nevertheless, the room should never be connected to the general airconditioning system because of the danger of mould and fungal spores being distributed throughout the building.

Fumigation room

The use of fumigation chambers is a most sensitive issue today. In the past they were provided as a matter of course. The difficulty is that the fumigant most commonly used was ethylene oxide, a gas now shown to be carcinogenic.[9]

While the gas is still available, if it is employed it should only be used under the most stringent conditions and by licensed and professional contractors.

If a fumigation chamber is to be included as part of your building design, it must have its own gas exhaust system. The floor of the room housing the chamber should have sufficient load bearing capacity to take the weight of the chamber and should be tiled. Again, there should be a drainage outlet.

In its Kwun Tong facility, the Public Records Office of Hong Kong has included a chamber and is planning to use a nitrogen based gas as the fumigant, one of the few institutions to adopt this method.[10]

Microfilming/reprography room

A dedicated area will be needed if you conduct a microfilming program (for example, on vital control records, or important records for access and preservation purposes or other special projects).

The area should incorporate space for microfilm cameras, film processing equipment, as well as the staff who are undertaking filming and specialised photographic work. If large amounts of film stock are to be stored on site, a cold storage unit will also be required.

Dark room

If photographic material is developed on site, a dark room will be needed. It should be fitted with a sink, fume extraction fan, safe lights and light trap entrance.

Special drainage will be needed to dispose of all chemical wastes. The room must, of course, be capable of complete darkness.

Materials store room

Given the nature of the chemicals used in conservation processes, there should be a room devoted to their secure storage. Chemicals can normally be stored in the flammable liquid cabinet in the wet area. However, large amounts of chemicals, over 20 litres, should be stored outside the building in an external flammable liquid store.

You should also be aware that there are regulations across the Australian States and Territories which govern the storage of hazardous substances and you may be required to obtain a permit to store some materials on site.

Office accommodation

Provision should also be made for office accommodation for conservation staff (staff accommodation will be discussed shortly), and possibly a small library.

Shelving and Storage Containers

With the high cost of storing records, it is imperative that you make the most efficient use of your storage areas to ensure the greatest quantity of records can be held in a finite amount of floor space. At the same time, there is a need to allow for ready access to the records and safe usage of the shelving by staff.

What follows is a very basic description of shelving systems available today. For more detailed information, you should consult the publication produced by the National Archives of Australia, Standards Australia and Standards New Zealand, *Guidelines for Mobile Shelving for Archives, Libraries and Museums*.[11]

Mechanically-assisted mobile shelving.

Mobile steel shelving

Most archival facilities use mobile steel shelving. Static shelving is available too, but, of course, uses considerably more floor space to store the same amount of material.

Wooden shelving is also available, both in static and mobile form. However, as the preservation of records is an obvious major requirement of archival storage, evaluation of the reactivity of materials used in mobile shelving components is essential. Steel shelving is recommended where conservation must have priority in order to avoid problems such as combustibility and possible leaching or 'outgassing' of harmful agents.[12]

Mobile shelving is available with a number of different operational systems, the two most popular being mechanically assisted and electrically operated. Mechanically assisted shelving is found in most facilities. It allows the operator to move large masses of material with relative ease. These systems are operated by means of a handle or 'steering wheel' attached to the end of each row.

Electrically operated systems are the most convenient for staff to use, being operated by the simple push of a button, yet they are also the most expensive.

Shelving is manufactured in a wide array of dimensions, the most common being:

height	1 875 mm, 2 175 mm, 2 375 mm and 2 475 mm;
width	450 mm, 900 mm;
depth	300 mm, 400 mm and 500 mm.

These dimensions do not include the height of the mobile bases.

The National Archives of Australia has adopted standard units which are 2 475 mm high, 900 mm wide and 400 mm deep. This enables the provision of eight shelves per bay and allows for the storage of material such as standard files, registers, folders, books and index cards.

Many other institutions have the same width and depth ratios as the National Archives, but their heights vary dramatically. Shelving can, of course, go much higher. Ten-high, 12-high and even 14-high units are not uncommon. While enormous quantities of material can be housed in this type of high shelving, there may well be staff resistance to their usage and there are occupational health and safety aspects to consider.

Ultra-high shelving, say 30 or 40 shelves, may also present an added fire risk. With such shelving there is the possibility that if a fire begins near floor levels, the water from your sprinkler system may not be able to reach the flames and extinguish them. If you are considering the use of such shelving, you should check the extinguishing capacity of your sprinkler system carefully with fire safety experts beforehand.

Shelving is available for the storage of unboxed items such as magnetic tapes and films. Magnetic tapes can be stacked upright and held separately by means of thin stainless steel rods which run through each shelf and are connected at the top and bottom of each unit.

Film canisters are generally laid flat and stacked on top of each other, three or four high. Ideally, they should be stored individually, but if they must be stacked it is suggested that all shelves be arranged in a lop-sided fashion, with the front of the shelf one level higher than the back. The tilting effect helps to counter the possibility of items sliding forward during operation of the shelving.

There has been a recent innovation with the introduction of 'pizza' style shelving by a number of institutions and which is also being used by the National Archives at its Villawood repository for the storage of film. There are no shelves, only brackets attached to the uprights. The canisters are held in place horizontally by these brackets, which are placed on either side. Holes in the uprights mean that the brackets can be adjusted to accommodate different sized canisters. The canisters are held individually, not stacked on top of each other. Access to each canister is readily permitted and there is no possibility that a canister might slide off the brackets as the shelving moves.

If models or other large, bulky objects are to be stored, then a variety of commercial options are available. A number of firms provide racking in a variety of materials and sizes which can accommodate these items. Again, individual shelves are adjustable. Dust covers can also be installed to protect the items. Some types of racking can also be placed onto mobile bases if desired. The National Archives has installed mobile racking in its Adelaide, South Australia, repository to house large volumes of synoptic charts produced by the Bureau of Meteorology.

For objects which are particularly fragile, such as large architectural models or glass plate negatives, it may be preferable to use stationary shelving for extra protection from breakage or damage.

Plan cabinets (usually six or ten-drawer) are recommended for drawings, plans, charts and posters. Such material is best stored flat, rather than rolled, with archival quality paper interleaved between items. The cabinets can be placed in static formation or they can be stacked on top of each other and placed on mobile bases. In this way, they operate in precisely the same way as mobile shelving.

How high to stack the cabinets is subject to debate. British Standard (BS) 5454 states that 1 400 mm is the maximum desirable height.[13] This would permit two cabinets only (as they are generally about 550 mm high) and would add considerably to the overall floor space that would be needed. Yet it must be said that the greater the height, the more resistance there will be from staff who have to use the cabinets. There is an additional problem involving high units whereby the weight of the cabinets bearing down upon each other can cause the frames of the lower cabinets to warp, even if only slightly. The result is that drawers on the lower cabinets can slip out of their runners.

Three cabinets high (about 1 650 mm plus the height of the mobile base) would seem to be the best compromise for maximising storage capacity, permitting ease of access and protecting the records themselves.

If the decision is made to go higher, mobile platforms and other safety measures will need to be put in place for staff to use when they are accessing material on the higher shelves. In any event, it is a wise move to place high usage material on the lower shelves.

Cantilevered racking is also available for exceptionally long drawings. The units can be coupled to each other with the only limitation then being the size of your storage area. In this respect, the Queensland State Archives has developed a system which can store drawings and plans many metres in length.[14] The National Archives also uses racking to hold railway drawings over 10 metres in length in its Rosny Park (Hobart, Tasmania) facility.

A number of manufacturers also provide decorative end panels which are placed over the uprights adjacent to the principal point of entry to the mobile installation. They are aesthetically pleasing and have the effect of reducing the harsh visual appearance caused by large expanses of steel shelving.

Designing the shelving layout and the placement of shelving units on the master plan

In locating each shelving unit on a master drawing, a number of factors must be taken into account. These will include wheelchair access, if appropriate, widths of major access aisles and fire corridors. You should leave sufficient space for the opening of doors into storage areas and for the movement of staff pushing large trolleys. Sufficient space should also be left to allow rapid access to fire exits.

One of the most difficult issues is establishing just how much mobile shelving will actually fit into an available floor area. Or put another way, how do you convert square floor metres into linear shelf metres? The National Archives has developed a number of formulae in response to this dilemma:

- 1 square metre of open storage area will accommodate 12 linear metres of storage if 8-high (2 475 mm) mobile shelving is used.
- 1 square metre of open storage area will accommodate 10 linear metres of storage if 6-high (1 875 mm) mobile shelving is used.
- 1 square metre of open storage area will accommodate 7 linear metres of storage if 8-high (2 475 mm) static shelving is used.

These ratios are averages and are intended to give guidance only.

The location of all obstructions should, of course, be carefully noted when designing a shelving layout. They might include pillars, skirting boards, airconditioning intakes (in the walls or the floor), power outlets, light switches and sensors, fire hose reels and fire extinguishers.

If there are pillars in the storage areas (and ideally their numbers should be kept to a minimum), they should serve as the starting point when placing units on a design drawing. Remaining shelving is then placed in position working outwards from the pillars.

Calculating the true length and depth of mobile shelving units

Length

When calculating the length and width of each mobile block, there are several factors which you should not overlook. The first is the true depth of each row. While shelves may be 400 mm deep, they are fixed inside uprights which are themselves 430 mm deep. This results in the block being longer than you might at first think.

The second factor to account for is the moveable aisleway. Where normal sized containers are involved, 1 000 mm is sufficient. Where larger sized items are involved, such as plans, drawings or volumes, a deeper aisleway will be needed – possibly up to 1 500 mm or even wider.

The easiest means of calculating the length of a block is to multiply the number of rows by the upright width and then add in the moveable aisleway. If a unit consists of 12 rows (regardless of whether they are 12 single-sided or 6 double-sided rows), where each row is 430 mm deep, then the length of the block will be:

12 rows x 430 mm	=	5 160 mm
Moveable aisleway	=	1 000 mm
Total	=	6 160 mm

Width

To calculate the width of a unit, multiply the number of bays in each row by their width (usually 900 mm). Then add the operating mechanism (handle or 'steering wheel') which is usually about 185 mm. For example, if each row is five bays wide, the total width will be :

Five bays x 900 mm   =   4 500 mm
Operating mechanism =   185 mm (approximately)
Total   =   4 685 mm

Fire safety

The installation of mobile shelving can jeopardise an area's fire safety unless you have taken appropriate precautions. The location of emergency and exit light fittings should be noted. After the shelving has been installed, the lights may require relocation if they are no longer visible, or additional signage alerting staff of their existence.

The accessibility of fire exits may also be affected and their adequacy should be confirmed with authorities, as should the location of fire extinguishers and hose reels.

Storage containers

Over the past 30 years, most institutions have adopted a series of standard containers in which to store their records, and abandoned earlier practices of having items simply left on the shelves or wrapped in bundles. Containers provide greater protection and assist with the ease of movement of records.

Some institutions may still leave items loose on shelves. This is a highly undesirable practice. It makes material more vulnerable to dust (even if you have a good filtration system), light and insects. Wrapping items in paper and tying them with string is a clumsy, time consuming and antiquated practice.

Until recently, most containers were produced from recycled paper materials. Generally, the containers were not solid, but consisted of two layers of paper with a piece of fluted board in between. Using fluted materials reduced costs, yet still gave the containers considerable strength.

Higher quality, archival materials have been available for some time but were considerably more expensive as they were usually made from solid materials, rather than fluted. Their costs generally prevented their use on a broad scale.

Recently, the National Archives entered into a joint venture with several paper and board manufacturers/fabricators for the development and production of a wide array of containers produced from archival quality, fluted materials. The result has seen the introduction of a range of containers which ensure that permanent value materials are afforded greater protection and at reasonable costs. The containers can house standard files, index cards, computer printouts, audio and video cassettes, magnetic tapes, books and drawings. Old technology, such as gramophone recordings, and new technology, such as compact discs, are also accommodated. The new range of archival containers is not just restricted to the National Archives; they are available commercially.

Storage containers are also manufactured from other materials, most commonly polypropylene, which is an inert plastic. It is an ideal medium for film and tape storage as it will not rust. In the past, films and tapes were often held in metal canisters which were prone to rusting.

Archival quality containers and packaging materials

A word of warning concerning the terms 'archival quality' and 'acid-free'. They have been used quite liberally in recent times in various forms of advertising for containers and packaging materials, but you need to exercise some caution.

**TABLE 6 NATIONAL ARCHIVES OF AUSTRALIA
CONTAINER TYPES, USES AND DIMENSIONS**

Type	Record Format	Outside Dimensions (in millimetres)
Type 1	Foolscap files and video cassettes	389 × 259 × 174
Type 2	Foolscap files (the container is only half as wide as a type and is used for small consignments)	389 × 259 × 85
Type 3	Small index cards, audio cassettes and microfilms	389 × 121 × 165
Type 4	Folders and registers	389 × 259 × 290
Type 5	Large index cards	389 × 146 × 216
Type 6	Computer printouts	316 × 125 × 428
Type 8	Rolled plans and drawings (AO size)	870 × 109 × 109
Type 9	Bank cheques	389 × 197 × 112
Type 10	X-rays and large documents	389 × 121 × 425
Type 12	Large gramophone recordings (10, 12 inch)	343 × 339 × 86
Type 13	Small gramophone recordings (7 inch)	225 × 208 × 86
Type 14	Large gramophone recordings (16 inch)	445 × 441 × 86
Type 16	Microfiche	218 × 121 × 165

If you are purchasing paper products, you should ensure that they are indeed archival quality. They should be alkaline, made from the highest grade lignin-free pulp and exhibit sufficient strength to accommodate the records held within.

If you are purchasing products for photographic storage, then materials such as polypropylene, polyethylene or uncoated polyester, eg (*Mylar-D*™) are the most appropriate. You should ascertain if the products are described as 'copy safe' or 'photo safe'.[15]

Staffing and Public Areas

An archives building is not just for the storage of records, though that is its primary function. The building will be home to staff, visitors and the public too. Planning spatial layouts for people is just as important as it is for records.[16]

Staffing areas

When planning the layout of staffing areas, there are many factors that you should take into consideration. Provision will not only need to be made for your staff, but also their furniture and equipment, eg desks, chairs, computers, bookshelves and filing cabinets. Some staff may also require a small quantity of static or mobile shelving to house support material.

There will need to be provision for conference rooms, training rooms and, possibly, private meeting rooms for interviews and confidential discussions. Of course, such private rooms will need to be soundproofed. Designated work areas may be needed for staff engaged on group projects.

Space will need to be allowed for registries, storerooms and possibly a library. If the library is a large one, and mobile shelving is being used to house this material, the floor loadings should, of course, be sufficient to take the weight.

Last, there are likely to be general areas such as an amenities room, sick room and rest rooms.

A few points can now be made about designing a layout to accommodate these areas.

First, in placing sections and departments on a draft master plan, workflows should be recognised, so that sections which work in close cooperation are located adjacent to each other. Conversely, staff should not have to pass through one working area, disrupting people as they go, in order to get to another work area. Staff dealing with the public should be as close as possible to the reading room.

You should make the maximum use of whatever natural light is available. Give the benefits of windows to as many people as possible, though curtains or blinds may be necessary depending on heat gain and glare. It is preferable that individual offices are not placed next to the windows. If offices are placed against the windows, glass partitioning should be used to allow natural light to pass into the staffing areas.

Attention should be paid to cables – telephones, computers, printers – as they can represent a safety hazard. They should be appropriately housed in conduits, around skirting boards or against pillars and poles.

When calculating spatial allocations for each member of staff, remember to allow not only for their furniture and equipment but circulation spaces as well. This is especially important in large, open plan areas where staff will not only need to be able to move around their own area but also move easily to meet with other staff.

All staff should be consulted and kept informed during the design phase. It may also be desirable to consult with staff unions and other groups too, eg occupational health and safety committees. The rationale for whatever layout is being proposed should be clearly explained. So too should the basis of whatever spatial allocation formula has been developed, particularly what it does and does not include.

You should remember that work space is a very personal thing and that many people become very attached to, and quite emotional about, their own space. You do need to consult and be reasonably sensitive to the wants and demands of others. Yet this reasonableness must be tempered. You may have to remind staff that there is a limited budget, and probably a limited time frame. So the consultation period needs to have clearly defined parameters which should be explained at the outset.

You may also find that staff who have been in less than satisfactory accommodation for some time may want to recreate what they have in the new building, albeit on a larger and more modern scale. What is sometimes overlooked is the opportunity a new building provides to critically review work practices and work flows. It may pay you to encourage staff to rethink what they do, and how they do it, and whether things can be done differently.

Creature comforts

In planning an office layout, there are a number of basic requirements that must also be taken into consideration. The first is thermal comfort, a general term referring to temperature and relative humidity levels and the quality of the air itself. Generally speaking, for Australian conditions, a summer temperature range of 23°–26° Celsius and a winter range of 20°–24° Celsius is desirable, as is a relative humidity level of 40%–60%.[17]

Where staff and visitors work regularly, there should be an illumination level of between 240 lux and 400 lux at the desktop level.[18] Appropriate lighting is particularly relevant given the recent rapid proliferation of computers and terminals, which are now constantly used by staff at their desks and the public in reading rooms. Reflections from computer screens and nearby expanses of glass may need to be countered by anti-glare devices.

Noise levels can be distracting and should be kept to a minimum. Noisy, obstructive machines such as photocopiers and printers should be placed in corners out of the way or in small rooms by themselves.

If there is a large open area housing many people, it may be necessary to use low height partitioning, screens, artificial pot plants or other means to reduce noise levels and also give each member of staff some privacy.

Public areas

Public areas should be located near the main entrance to the building and should be secured from the remainder of the building. It should not be possible for a visitor to walk unchallenged into a general staffing area and certainly not into the record storage areas.

It is generally the case that members of the public will pass through a reception point at the entrance and then into the reading room.

When designing research facilities, you need to remember that some readers:
- will want to work quietly at a table by themselves;
- will work as a group and want to discuss their research as they go – this is particularly the case with readers engaged in family history research;
- may be using microfilm readers which can be quite noisy (particularly when operating in high speed forward or reverse);
- may be searching through hard copy finding aids, indexes and packing lists, spreading material around them while they search;
- may work at computer terminals searching databases;
- may want to type their notes directly onto a laptop computer or dictate their notes onto a tape recorder;
- may want to access audiovisual records, eg films or sound recordings, and will need a quiet area for this; and
- may be using large format records, such as maps or plans, and will need ample space for this.

So, depending on how many readers visit your facility, and the level of staff and funding available, your reading room needs to cater for all of these activities. In essence, multiple reading rooms are needed, or a single room which allows all of these functions to co-exist.

First, there needs to be a basic reading room to allow readers to peruse documents. The room should be fitted with tables and chairs. There may possibly be a large table for maps and a lectern-style table for large volumes. An area should be set aside for group research – a table which can accommodate four or five persons.

Another area, either a separate room or an alcove, should be set aside for finding aids, whether they be in hard copy or computerised form.

Noisy machines, such as microfilm readers, should be screened off from other areas. Private booths or carrels may need to be provided for readers using their own computers and tape

The public reading room at the National Archives' new headquarters at East Block in Parkes, Canberra.
Photograph by Barry Brown.

recorders. Remember to allow for sufficient power outlets, particularly for computers. A theatrette may also be needed to allow the playback of audiovisual materials.

A small interview room should be included to enable staff to meet with first time readers coming to grips with records, finding aids and methods of operation.

All rooms and areas should be clearly signposted. Similarly, all finding aids should be identified plainly.

Obviously, all of these rooms or areas will require close supervision. Depending on how many staff are available, it may be necessary to use cameras and possibly mirrors. If separate rooms are provided it may be desirable to use glass partitioning.

There are other facilities that readers will require. A place to store their bags, coats and umbrellas, as well as an amenities room as they should not be permitted to bring food or drink into the reading room.

If your institution has an exhibition and marketing program, dedicated areas will be needed for these purposes. The exhibition area will require special lighting, security and airconditioning controls.

A small shop may be needed to display the items that your institution has produced for sale.

General ambience

The general ambience of the public areas should also be taken into consideration. It is, after all, how the public perceives you. The use of colours, fabrics, materials and furniture are all important. They should be designed to enhance the aesthetic and functional appeal of the area, not detract from it, nor make it overpowering or confusing. In this context, it also is desirable that as much natural light as possible be allocated to reader areas.

Noise levels should be kept to a minimum. Curtains and carpets are a good way to absorb noise. Floors with hard surfaces – slate or vinyl – while they may be ideal in a foyer, are not recommended in reading areas due to the noise factor. Noise can have many sources – readers distracting each other, staff distracting readers, external noises, nearby plant rooms or traffic. If the reading room is adjacent to a main road, it may be necessary to have all windows in the room double-glazed.

Tables and chairs should be ergonomically based, ie have adjustable height settings, and be comfortable to sit on and work at.

Again, thermal comfort should be taken into consideration, the same general conditions applying as for the staffing areas.

And last, pay attention to artificial lighting levels. Generally, they should be the same as for the staffing areas.

Occupational Health and Safety

It is generally expected of a modern repository that it not only be environmentally friendly but that it should make a positive commitment to the safety of staff and visitors.[19] In 1991 this was recognised by the Australian Government with the passage of the *Occupational Health and Safety (Commonwealth Employment) Act*.

Many institutions, whether government or privately operated, now have a duty of care to provide a safe and comfortable working environment for their staff and visitors to their establishments. A number of these responsibilities are outlined in the publication *Officewise: A guide to health and safety in the office*.[20]

A variety of safety issues affect the purpose-built repository of today. This is not surprising given the size of some of these facilities and the types of activities undertaken within them. There are numerous potential dangers which may be found in older buildings, and which may come to prominence if an attempt is made convert an existing facility for use as a repository as was briefly mentioned in chapter 2. Two dangers, in particular, are polychlorinated biphenyls and asbestos.

Polychlorinated biphenyls (PCBs) were used in capacitors in fluorescent light fittings installed up to the mid-1970s. They have been found in a number of National Archives' facilities, eg Villawood and East Victoria Park (Western Australia), and have since been removed.

The dangers of asbestos have been well documented. Asbestos was often used as part of the lagging in airconditioning ducts or as insulation in fire doors. Provided the material is contained, there is generally no cause for alarm. However, problems occur when loose material can escape from confined spaces. Removing asbestos is a specialised and costly task.

Another danger which has emerged in recent times is legionnaires' disease. It is particularly of relevance to those institutions which use cooling towers as part of their airconditioning systems. Legionella bacteria develops in warm, humid conditions. As such, it is not confined to cooling towers but can also thrive in humidifiers, ducting and even hot water systems. As knowledge of this disease has expanded, so too have your responsibilities and you must ensure that cooling towers in particular are regularly inspected, cleaned and detailed records kept. In most Australian States, substantial penalties can be enforced if this is not done.

A potential danger occurs when buildings or records themselves are fumigated. Building fumigation is considered in more detail in chapter 6. Whether it should be undertaken at all is hotly debated, but when it is it should only be done in special circumstances and only by trained contractors and should never become a routine event.

There are other dangers too, but perhaps not quite as exotic as asbestos or legionnaires' disease. Large storage areas with expanses of high shelving accessed daily by staff present a number of materials handling issues. All staff should, of course, be trained in the safe handling of equipment, how to retrieve items from high shelving and how to safely operate mobile shelving.

Some records may themselves represent a danger, eg degrading films can give off strong acids which can cause skin and eye problems; older records may have been treated with (and contain residues of) pesticides that are now known to be highly toxic. Also, people who are prone to allergic reactions may be affected by dust and particles generated as records degrade. These problems can usually be managed by provision of personal protective equipment such as coats, gloves, goggles and masks, and by maintaining a clean work environment with good ventilation.

Occupational health and safety issues are likely to impact further on archival repositories, and their effects will continue to be felt by those who design these buildings and those who work in them.

Sick Building Syndrome

In recent years, the term 'Sick Building Syndrome' has come into vogue. Opinions vary widely, from those who maintain that the concept is real and buildings do make people sick, to those who assert that it does not exist, that it is all in the mind. Some would ignore it, while others would tear down a building to overcome it.

As with so many things, the truth usually lies somewhere in between. A facility's internal conditions and the materials from which it is built can cause allergies which may manifest themselves in the form of headaches, sore throats, running noses and coughing. The explanation for some of these symptoms may be quite simple.

Ideal working conditions include thermal comfort and air quality. Thermal quality does not only mean appropriate temperature and humidity levels, but a regular supply of fresh air. If there is insufficient fresh air entering the building's airconditioning system, or if the movement of air throughout the building is outside recommended levels, this will cause health problems.

The facility's airconditioning filters should be inspected, cleaned and replaced when necessary. Likewise, the airconditioning ducts need to regularly inspected and cleaned; the cleaning taking place every 10 years. It is an expensive task, but if left undone the build up of dust and other contaminants can certainly lead to health problems.

If the decision is made not to cover the floors in the storage areas, and to use bare concrete instead, the surface should be treated, otherwise contaminants may be released and enter the airconditioning system. And, of course, there is the risk of damage to the records too.

Furniture and furnishings can give rise to allergies. Woollen fabric on chairs may release fibres. Certain types of furniture, eg plastic chairs, can give off odours. Carpets can likewise trap dust and release fibres.

Excessive light from overhead fittings or glare reflecting from computer screens, windows or partitions can give rise to headaches.

Excessive noise can cause discomfort and illness. Noise from the airconditioning system, or even nearby items such as photocopiers or printers, can be extremely irritating.

So, it can be seen that the explanation for staff complaints and illnesses does not have to rely on something as exotic as Sick Building Syndrome. The answer can, in many cases, be quite simple.

Facilities for the disabled

In providing a safe and comfortable environment for staff and visitors, it needs to be remembered that a modern purpose-built repository can provide many hazards for the disabled and provision needs to be made for them too.[21]

You should ensure that wheelchair facilities are available both outside the building and within. Reserved car spaces should be provided, clearly marked with the disabled logo and they should be located close to the main entrance. If there are steps leading to the entrance, a ramp should be included as well. The ramp should be wide enough to accommodate wheelchairs, preferably without tight corners. The entrance door handles (assuming the doors are not automatic) should not be so high that a person in a wheelchair cannot reach them.

Special provision will need to be made inside the building, both for staff and visitors to the facility. Again, doors should be wide enough to allow the passage of wheelchairs. Door handles and light switches should not be too high that they cannot be reached. It may be necessary to provide a rest room which is fitted out specifically for use by disabled people. Reception counters should not be so high that they are intimidating to persons in wheelchairs. The tables and chairs in the reading room should be able to comfortably accommodate disabled readers.

Hearing- or sight-impaired people should also be taken into consideration. They may require provision of special phones to enable them to communicate or enlarging equipment to enable them to read documents.

Last, remember to allow for disabled persons when you are devising your emergency evacuation procedures.

1   The section on special purpose storage areas has been prepared with the assistance of internal working documents, specifications and notes prepared by the National Archives´ Facilities Program.
2   The section on conservation laboratories has been written with the advice and assistance of staff from the National Archives' Preservation Program.
3   Christopher Kitching, *Archive Buildings in the United Kingdom 1977–1992*, London, 1993, pp. 66–67; Vicki Warden, 'The New Queensland State Archives building', paper presented to the Conference of the Australian Society of Archivists, Townsville, May 1994, p. 51.
4   Derek Ballantyne, 'Conservation areas in the new building of the National Archives of Canada', *Janus*, 1995, 2, p. 95.
5   Vicki Warden, paper presented to the Conference of the Australian Society of Archivists, p. 51.
6   Verbal advice to the author, March 1997.
7   Australian Standard 1680.1-1990 *Interior Lighting Part 1: General Principles and Recommendations*, Sydney, 1990, p. 16.
8   Standards Australia has produced a series of standards relating to constructing a laboratory and laboratory safety, ie AS/NZS2982.1-1997 *Laboratories and Construction – General requirements*, Sydney, 1997 and AS2243.1-9, 1990-1997 Safety in Laboratories, Sydney, 1990–1997.
9   Numerous references to the dangers involving ethylene oxide will be found in the *Ethylene Oxide User's Guide* located on the Internet (www.ethyleneoxide.com).
10   Verbal advice to the author, March 1997.
11   National Archives, Standards Australia and Standards New Zealand, *Guidelines for Mobile Shelving for Archives, Libraries and Museums*, Sydney, 1997. The *Guidelines* are a lay person's guide to mobile steel shelving. They describe various systems, and their operating components, and show how to design a typical shelving layout over a large floor area.
12   British Standard (BS) 5454, *Recommendations for Storage and Exhibition of Archival Documents*, London, 1989, p. 7 and Mary Lynn Ritzenthaler, *Archives and Manuscripts: Conservation: A Manual on Physical Care and Management*, Society of American Archivists, Chicago, 1983, p. 38.
13   British Standard (BS) 5454, p. 8.
14   Vicki Warden, paper presented to the Conference of the Australian Society of Archivists, p. 52.
15   Guy Petherbridge, 'Environmental and housing considerations for the preservation of modern records – a guide for the records manager', *Proceedings of the 8th National Convention of the Records Management Association of Australia*, Darwin, 1991, p. 137, footnote 20 and National Archives of Australia Archives Advice 10 Caring for Your Family Archive, 1997 and Archives Advice 11 Archival Quality Packaging, 1997.
16   Much useful material in designing an office layout will be found in the publication *Officewise: A guide to health and safety in the office*, Comcare Australia OHS Book 1, Canberra, 1996.
17   *Airconditioning and thermal comfort in Australian Public Service offices*, Comcare Australia, Canberra, 1994, pp. 22–26.
18   Australian Standard 1680.1-1990, p.16.
19   The section on occupational health and safety has been prepared with the assistance of internal working documents, specifications and notes prepared by the National Archives´ Facilities Program.
20   Comcare Australia, *Officewise: A guide to health and safety in the office*.
21   Two sources which contain useful information on providing services for disabled persons are: Australian Standard 1428.1-4 1992–1993, *Design for Access and Mobility*, Sydney, 1992–1993 and Brenda Beasley Kepley, 'Archives: accessibility for the disabled', *American Archivist*, vol. 46, no. 1, 1983, pp. 42–51.

Chapter 5
Building the Building

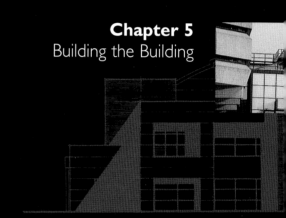

EAST

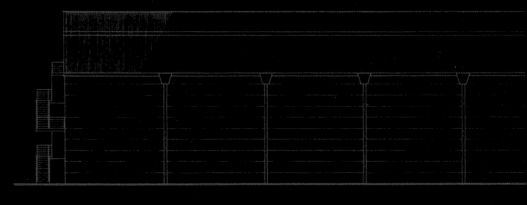

SOUTH

Preparing the Way

To any who soon may be planning
a new archival building, may I say
that you will find it to be an
interesting and challenging task.[1]

Writing the design brief and working with professionals

The professionals with whom you are dealing will probably have never been involved in designing and constructing a purpose-built repository. On more than one occasion, there have been reports of architects and engineers chosen to undertake this type of work having to use the dictionary to ascertain what archives actually are before they could even begin the project.[2]

For this reason, from the outset they must understand that what is being sought is a facility for the permanent preservation of archival material in varying physical formats, access to some of this material by members of the public and a comfortable and safe working environment for staff. And furthermore:

- it is not a library;
- it is not a museum; and
- it is not an art gallery.

But, like these buildings, it does have its unique set of special requirements.

The integrated preservation aspects of the building must be emphasised repeatedly, and so too must the need for strict and constantly sustainable environmental conditions. If there is one factor which has gone horribly wrong in the past, it is this.

In order to convey what is truly needed, a functional design brief must be prepared. This is the document which will set out your requirements and ensures that the professionals with whom you will be working – such as architects and builders – have a clear and concise understanding of those requirements.[3]

During the preparation of the brief, you will need to ask a number of very basic questions. The answers not only help shape the brief, they determine what kind of building will ultimately be delivered and whether it will fully satisfy your needs.

Design and designing

A typical purpose-built repository usually has five principal areas or zones:

- records storage – the largest area, which may include a number of specialised compartments, such as low temperature and security vaults;
- staffing – offices, conference/training facilities, registry, library, amenities;
- reference facilities – public and official reading rooms, libraries, exhibitions;
- special services – preservation, reprography, bookbinding and repair; and
- building services – plant rooms, loading docks, store rooms.

The design brief should start with a general outline about your institution and the type of building you are seeking. It should incorporate descriptions in plain English of what is needed and why. This should then be followed by a general summary of major space requirements.

Abridged version of the introduction to the brief prepared by the National Archives for its East Burwood repository in 1991[4]

The National Archives is responsible for the broad management of the whole body of records of the Commonwealth Government in order to meet the proper needs of the government and the public. These records have been created as part of the functions of the agencies of the Commonwealth Government in their day to day operations. Many records are of permanent or long-term value. They are, in some cases, of historical or cultural value. In other cases, they are of evidential value or are needed to enable agencies to carry out their obligations and responsibilities. They may also enable members of the public to pursue their legal rights or occupational needs. Such records are, therefore, unique and irreplaceable. There is a large and constantly increasing volume of records in a wide variety of materials and formats.

In order for the National Archives to achieve the efficient management of Commonwealth records in its custody, the aim is to maintain records in the best condition possible by provision of optimum storage conditions for each type of record.

To this end, it is proposed to construct a purpose-built records repository which will provide up to date, climate-controlled, secure storage facilities. Records will primarily be paper, audiovisual or in magnetic format. Some provision is required for odd shaped objects such as plans, charts and models.

The building should be of a standard which reflects the fact that it houses permanent material. It should incorporate current construction and building system technology aimed at ensuring the longevity of records stored while minimising operating costs.

The building will be a single or two storey construction providing approximately 5 200 square metres of usable floor space. The design should include provision for future expansion for storage as well as office accommodation. In general, the building will need a capacity of approximately 45 000 shelf metres (4 000 square metres) for general storage purposes, with an additional 1 200 square metres for office accommodation, special facilities and incidentals.

Additional special purpose storage is to be provided for:
* mobile plan cabinets, static shelving and/or fixed racking for those items which cannot be stored in standard shelving, such as models and other large objects (250 square metres);
* security vault (100 square metres); and
* cold room/low temperature environment to house audiovisual material or computer tapes (150 square metres).

Shelving in all storage areas is to be mechanically assisted double-sided mobile units operating on a three-track configuration, with tracking being sunk into the floor and being flush with the floor when vinyl floor coverings are laid. Floor loadings in these areas should be sufficient to take the weight of fully laden mobile shelving units and is suggested to be a minimum of 12 kpa.

An area of 280 square metres is to be allowed for conservation and preservation facilities, which will include office space for staff. Three separate sections will be involved, comprising a laboratory (130 square metres), an airing room/box store (100 square metres) and a microfilming/reproduction room (50 square metres). Provision should also be made for a dark room.

It is estimated that approximately 20 staff would work in the building initially. The building will be accessed by members of the public and provision will need to be made for a reading room (400 square metres).

Office designs should be flexible to accommodate future growth and changes.

The design brief should then describe in detail the specific requirements of the building:

- building fabric – the need for a totally sealed and pest-free environment, using low maintenance materials;
- designated environmental conditions for all storage areas – temperature, relative humidity levels, air quality and lighting;
- energy management;
- fire protection – detection and suppression;
- security – external and internal measures;
- public access facilities;
- staffing facilities; and
- conservation facilities.

Your new building must cater to all of these requirements. Long after the building itself has ceased to function, hopefully many years into the future, the records it has housed will have survived in a satisfactory condition.

Now, regardless of what shape the building finally takes, a key factor in preparing a design brief is that work flows between each of the five areas must be fully recognised and understood and, of course, conveyed to the professionals. The final design should be such as to ensure the ability of each component of the building to function as part of a combined entity.

So, the brief should reflect all relevant work flows. It should show how the public areas interrelate with staffing, how the staffing areas interrelate with each other, how conservation facilities should be near the principal storage area, and so forth.

A simple schematic diagram may help at this point:

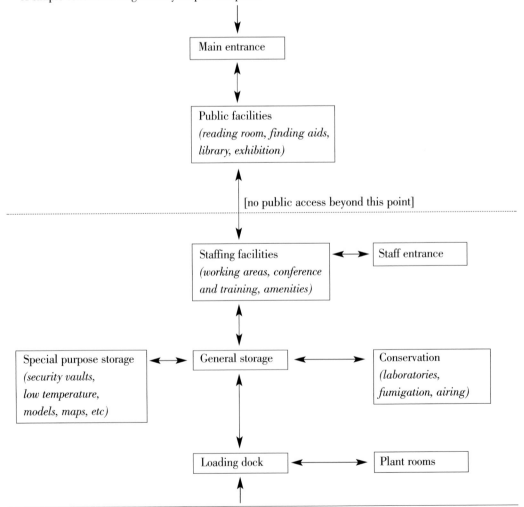

Solid, Safe, Secure: Building Archives Repositories in Australia

Work Flow Diagram

Public

The public will have access to limited areas of the building, such as the reading room, exhibition area and so on. Such areas should be located near the main entrance. The remainder of the building will be secured from public access, with occasional exceptions such as guided 'behind the scenes' tours.

Staff

Staff usually have a different entrance to the building. Some staff will have unlimited access to all areas of the building, while others will not. They may, for example, be restricted from the security vaults.

Records storage

The loading dock is where all records arrive at (and possibly leave from) the building. Records will be housed within different, but adjacent, areas of the building, usually depending on their physical format. They can of course be moved – they may be taken to conservation for repair or copying, or they can be taken into the public areas for consultation or display.

Conservation

Conservation facilities will usually be grouped together and within proximity of the major storage areas.

Plant rooms

The plant rooms will normally only be accessible by facilities management staff and maintenance contractors.

Design flexibility

There must also be a degree of flexibility built into every design. Office areas of the future will no doubt change, and it is always a good move to have partitions which can readily be adjusted. Allowances should also be made for alterations to cabling (computers, printers, telephones) should the need ever arise. In this context, College Park in the USA has used false floors throughout its office areas to house all cabling and to enable ready alteration in the future if needed.[5]

To help illustrate these points, the ground floor plan for the National Archives' East Burwood repository is shown overleaf. This graphically shows the relationship between the staffing and public areas and the location of all storage areas.

Last, it can be stated with some certainty that the final factor in the design phase is the careful study of all documentation and repeated consultation with the architects, builders and planning authorities to ensure that everything has been clearly understood and put into effect.

If these factors are given due consideration at the design phase, the final product will have fewer problems than might otherwise be the case.

Now, it should be recognised that the functional brief is simply the starting point for the project. The next stage involves working closely with the design developers and each of the technical disciplines (eg mechanical engineers) to prepare detailed documentation used as part of the tender package and ultimately to construct the building.

Storage capacities

One of the special tasks that must be fulfilled as part of the design brief is determining the storage capacity of the building. This capacity must be clearly ascertained at the outset. To do this, a number of questions need to be asked:

- what is the quantity of records already on hand?
- what quantities of records are likely to be transferred in the near future?
- what are the annual growth rates likely to be?
- what type of records will the building be required to house; will special storage areas be needed, eg film storage, security storage, areas for maps or models?

The National Archives works on the principle that a building's initial storage capacity should be of such a size as to comfortably accommodate all existing holdings and it should be capable of regular growth for at least another eight to ten years.

In the designing phase, it is crucial that you are aware of any storage backlogs which exist in agencies which may be released for transfer once your new facility has been commissioned. This is especially so if your institution has been unable to accept transfers for some time.

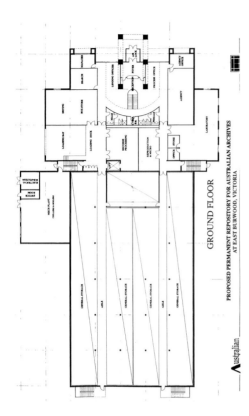

Architect´s drawings of the ground floor of the proposed respository for the East Burwood facility, Victoria.
Drawing produced by Australian Construction Service.

Storage areas must also be flexible, recognising that they must be able to accommodate changing record formats, both now and in the future. In this regard, adjustable shelving is very useful.

The building's future expansion potential must also be considered. Depending on which way you decide to grow, the building's structure and foundations must support this. This is especially relevant if it is likely that a decision will be made to build upwards in the future.

The Construction Process

With the completion of the design phase, the project will usually go to competitive tender and then comes the process of selecting the builder.

Selecting the builder

In many cases, the tendency is to pick the builder who submits the lowest quote for the work. While this is perhaps a natural tendency, price should be seen as one element only. Any builder who is being seriously considered for the construction of a purpose-built repository should be able to meet a number of selection criteria which include:

- clearly demonstrated experience with the construction of similar buildings;
- a proven reputation for completing projects on time;
- a proven reputation for completing projects within budget;
- a clearly demonstrated industrial record, as evidenced by minimum time lost due to union action;

- a clearly demonstrated safety record, as evidenced by a minimum number of accidents, complaints by staff, or investigations by safety committees;
- appropriately qualified staff available throughout the duration of the project; and
- a clear understanding of the outcome that is being sought.

This last criterion may seem rather trite, but if the builder cannot demonstrate that they understand what it is they are actually building, and the functions the building is intended to perform, then there is little point in awarding the contract to them, as the final product will more than likely not be what you wanted.

Each company which bids for the contract should be assessed against the above criteria. If there are any doubts, each should be rigorously questioned prior to the awarding of any contract.

Final selection should then be based on an interview process.

The project team

Once the contract has been let, a project team should then be assembled. The team will most likely comprise:
- the construction project manager;
- a site manager representing the builder;
- the architect;
- the archives project manager;
- a representative from the relevant government body (eg Department of Works); and
- specialist disciplines consulted as necessary.

The importance of good communication between members of this group can never be understated. Clearly defined lines of communication should be established at an early stage, thus ensuring that everyone is kept informed during the entire construction process.

As the project officer, you are responsible to your organisation but you will also be liaising regularly with the site manager of the construction company, the relevant architect and, if your organisation is a government body, a department of works (or similar).

The next step is to develop a clearly presented milestone chart. The chart should break the entire project into segments and list individual tasks, attributing these tasks to particular people and setting definitive time frames. Copies of the chart should, of course, be provided to all relevant parties. The important feature of a milestone chart is that it not only shows what is to happen, it shows who is responsible for making it happen and precisely when each event is to happen.

Now the work begins

Once the work begins, you should visit the site regularly. There should be site meetings attended by all members of the project team, giving each member the opportunity to report on progress to date and to air and resolve any difficulties that may have been encountered. A record of each meeting should be kept and made available to all interested groups.

Throughout the construction phase, it is a good idea for you to maintain a diary of all that happens, coupled with a photographic record. It is also a wise move to prepare a simple fact sheet which provides pertinent information and relevant statistics about the building and its construction schedule. From time to time, you will be called upon to provide a briefing, possibly to the head of the agency, or a government minister, or a distinguished visitor to the site. Having this information readily available, rather than having to prepare it in a rush, is always viewed favourably.

When things go wrong

Despite the best of intentions, you should accept the fact that, during the construction process, things will go wrong and these will need to be addressed. On a large-scale building project it would indeed be rare if this was not the case.

There can be many problems and frustrations. Contaminants may be discovered when clearing the site that had passed unnoticed during initial surveys. Construction holdups may arise due to industrial action, delays in supplies or as a result of bad weather.

You may be faced with changes to the design resulting in further delays. What looked good on paper suddenly does not work as well in reality. User groups may change their minds and request alterations to the plan.

The point here is not to despair over problems, but neither should you let them get out of hand. Brush fires should be attended to as quickly as possible and should never be allowed to turn into a major conflagration. The previously mentioned point about good communication comes to the fore here. It is vital that everyone be kept informed about the nature of the problem and what is being done to resolve it.

Industrial action and bad weather are beyond your control and, for the most part, simply have to be endured. Such obstacles will generally result in the builder seeking an extension to the initial contract completion date.

Changes to the master plan are another matter. The persons requesting the changes should be made fully aware that such changes will need to be assessed against likely delays and possible cost increases. It may be that the proposed changes will warrant an additional cost and extra time taken to implement them. Then again, changes should not be made on a whim and there needs to be sufficient justification for them to go ahead.

'As constructed' drawings and operational manuals

One of the requirements of any major construction is that, at the end of the project, you should be provided with a complete set of as constructed drawings (sometimes known by the title as completed or as built). It is often the case that builders are reluctant to devote time to this aspect of their work, simply because when they have finished one project they move on to the next and may not be as concerned as they should be with this matter.

The key point here is that the drawings are to be as constructed. Many changes can take place between the initial design phase and final construction. What you need is a record of the completed project, not the way it was going to be. This applies to all aspects of the project – architectural, civil, mechanical (airconditioning), electrical, hydraulic, fire and security.

In addition to drawings, a full set of operational manuals should also be provided. The manuals should clearly detail how systems such as airconditioning, fire and security are to be operated and maintained.

Having received the documents, it is vitally important that you keep them up to date. It is very easy to accept them at completion, put them away and then forget about them. Given that a typical archival repository has a life span of at least 50 years, and will undergo many changes in that time, the need for accurate drawings and manuals becomes obvious. Throughout its lifetime, the building's airconditioning system will probably be replaced. There will be changes brought about by new technology – such as lighting and fire systems – and these will require existing systems to be removed before the new ones can be installed. An extension may be added to the original building, and the builder will need to know where the current building's services are located.

Unless they have been kept up to date, it is very easy to find that after only a few years the drawings and manuals rapidly become obsolete and are of no use at all. It does not matter what format these items are in – whether paper, microfiche or electronic. They must be kept up to date and they must be readily accessible at all times.

Final inspection and acceptance

As the project nears completion, preparations will be made for a series of intense inspections and testing before the building is accepted. The inspections are normally undertaken by members of the project team, who will assess all parts of the building against the original design documentation and subsequently approved variations.

Before accepting the building, all systems should operate as per the specifications. All systems, eg airconditioning, fire, security and so on, will be brought into service and subjected to testing. The airconditioning system will undergo a final balance and conditions in the storage areas should then begin to stabilise. It is now vitally important that the nominated environmental conditions begin to be established and sustained, though it is usually the case that it will take some time for the system to settle in.

Prior to the letting of the contract, the builder will have been required to deposit a percentage of the total project cost with an approved third party (usually a bank) as a form of surety that the building will be completed within the designated time frame, unless extensions have been granted, and will meet the client's specifications. This surety is referred to as liquidated damages. It is held in trust for a set period after the project has been completed and is a means of guaranteeing that the builder will attend to any faults that may appear within that set period.

It is usually the case that a building will not pass inspection on its first attempt, and this is quite normal. As a result, a list of defects will be prepared for rectification by the builder. Generally, such items are quite minor. They might include doors that do not close properly, paint finishes on a wall that are imperfect or a few tears in some vinyl flooring. More often than not, there will normally be three or four inspections before the building is accepted.

Before you start bringing records into your new building, you should allow it the opportunity to acclimatise and 'breathe'. This simply means that the airconditioning system should be operating, nominated environmental conditions are being achieved and any contaminants left during the construction phase have been removed through the filtration system. It is suggested that you allow two weeks for this to happen.

Case Study Number 4 – Timeline: The Development of East Burwood

The timeline below shows the major steps involved in the design, construction and occupation of the East Burwood facility in Victoria. The entire process, from the time the National Archives first planned for the project until the official opening, took five years.

1989–1990	National Archives resolved to replace an existing, but totally unsuitable, facility at Brighton. Preliminary discussions were held with staff, unions, architects, Australian Construction Services (the Commonwealth Government's construction authority) and other parties. Some sketch work showing what form the new facility might take was prepared and some possible sites were examined. Initial costs of a new facility were also compiled.
mid 1990	The Department of Finance advised the National Archives that, in accordance with Commonwealth policy for projects of this size, a full cost benefit analysis would need to be undertaken. The analysis would assess an array of options, including the 'do nothing' option, and rank the costs, advantages and disadvantages of each option.
late 1990–1991	A cost benefit analysis was undertaken. Options assessed included refurbishing the Brighton facility; purchasing an existing facility and refurbishing it; constructing a new facility owned by the Commonwealth; having a developer construct a new facility and the National Archives leasing it; and doing nothing at all.
February 1991	Results of the cost benefit analysis demonstrated that the construction of a new facility with

outright ownership was the most favourable to the National Archives and to the Commonwealth.

May 1991 — The National Archives lodged a formal submission seeking Government funding in 1991/92 to purchase a new site and construct a purpose-built facility owned by the Commonwealth.

early-mid 1991 — A number of sites throughout Melbourne were considered and evaluated. A site at East Burwood showed considerable promise in terms of price and site selection requirements.

August 1991 — Funding was approved, subject to endorsement by the Parliamentary Standing Committee on Public Works. A total of $10.9 million was allocated to the project; in 1990/91 a small amount had already been advanced towards initial design costs. Funding would be provided over the next four years:
1991/92 $1.9 million (mainly for site acquisition);
1992/93 $4.0 million;
1993/94 $4.2 million; and
1994/95 $0.8 million;

September 1991 — The National Archives resolved to purchase the East Burwood site and a deposit was paid. Ownership of the site did not pass to the National Archives until 1992.

October 1991 — Functional design brief completed and preliminary sketch drawings undertaken. Construction of the facility estimated to cost $6.5 million.

December 1991 — Project referred to the Parliamentary Standing Committee on Public Works or PSCPW (note: all Commonwealth Government works projects in excess of $6 million must be approved by this Committee).

January 1992 — Detailed design documentation (specifications and drawings) continued.

February 1992 — PSCPW hearings conducted.

March 1992 — PSCPW approval given for the project.

May 1992 — Tenders called for construction of the facility at East Burwood.

July 1992 — Contract awarded to Prentice Builders Limited.

August 1992 — Project commenced, the first task involving earthworks, ie clearing the site and preparing the foundations.

October 1993 — Construction completed, the building inspected and handed over to the National Archives.

November 1993 — Transfer of records to the new building began and continued into 1994.

February 1994 — Official opening ceremony.

August 1994 — Brighton site handed back to the Commonwealth for ultimate disposal.

1   Kenneth W Richards, 'New Jersey's new archival facilities', *American Archivist*, vol. 27, no. 4, 1964, p. 489.
2   N O Wright, 'What the construction company needs to know about archives', *American Archivist*, vol. 27, no. 4, 1964, p. 495.
3   There are a number of sources which provide useful information on writing a design brief, eg: Lionel Bell, 'The archivist and his accommodation', *Archivaria*, 8, 1979, pp. 85–86; Michel Duchein, *Archive Buildings and Equipment*, Munich, 1988, pp. 141–154; and Christopher Kitching, *Archive Buildings in the United Kingdom 1977–1992*, London, 1993, pp. 72–74. The importance of good communication with your architect is emphasised by many authors including: Wolf Buchmann, 'Planning an archive building: the cooperation between architect and archivist', *Mitteilungen des Oesterreichischen Staatarchivs, Festschrift fuer Rolf Neck*, 1986, volume 39, pages 202–217 (this article was reproduced, in German, in *Archivum*, volume 31, 1988, pp. 27–36) Michel Duchein, *Archive Buildings and Equipment*, p. 28; Victor Gondos, 'Collaboration between archivists and architects in planning archives buildings', *Buildings and Equipment for Archives*, Bulletin of the National Archives, no. 6, Washington, 1944, pp. 9–21; and Robert A Schoenberner, 'What the architect needs to know about archives', *American Archivist*, vol. 27, no. 4, 1964, pp. 491–493.
4   National Archives, *Functional Brief for the Construction of a Purpose-built Repository for Australian Archives, Victoria*, Melbourne, Victoria, 1991, pp. 2–3.
5   Michele F Pacifico, 'The National Archives at College Park', *Government Information Quarterly*, vol. 13, no. 2, 1996. p. 119.

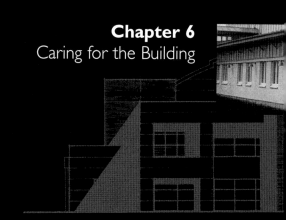

Chapter 6
Caring for the Building

EAST

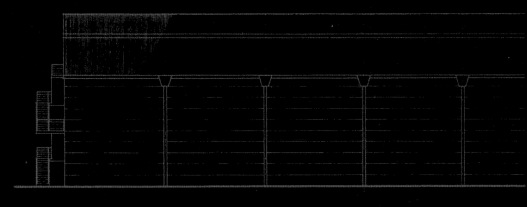

SOUTH

When the building is completed, it will have to be cared for.

After all, it will more than likely be there for the next 50 years and will be protecting records and providing a working environment for staff and visitors throughout that time.

Maintenance

It is often thought that maintenance begins following the completion and handover of the facility, but in truth it starts well before that. It begins as part of the building's overall design, which should include the requirement that it is constructed from low maintenance materials.

Once the repository is in operation, a comprehensive maintenance program needs to be put into place. Given the sophistication of modern facilities, and the number of systems which help run them, the importance of an ongoing maintenance program should not be underestimated. It is recognised that maintenance can be time consuming and costly, but to avoid it or reduce it in favour of other priorities will more than likely prove to be short-sighted and a very false economy.

Contracting out of maintenance

As technology has changed, and buildings evolved, so too has the way in which maintenance programs are developed. It is no longer the case that you simply select a contractor (often the relevant government works authority) and entrust maintenance to that contractor without any input on your part.

In recent years there has been an emerging trend to outsource maintenance activities. Many companies are available to do this work, and it is not uncommon for institutions to enter into comprehensive maintenance contracts with these companies. A maintenance framework should be developed which ensures that your new building will always provide the conditions necessary for records protection, and an appropriate environment for staff and visitors. Whichever contractor is chosen for the work, your principal object should be to obtain a comprehensive contract which is based on the contractor's continued good performance, which is simple to administer and, in addition, places the primary responsibility for the performance and condition of the facility upon the contractor.[1]

Maintenance philosophy and objectives

You should seek to develop a preventative service based on cyclic maintenance and inspection schedules. The aim should be to minimise the frequency of emergency call-outs, to allow maintenance tasks to be planned and to ensure that these tasks are scheduled to synchronise with normal operations, in order to lower overall running costs.

You should request that the preventative maintenance plan to be implemented by the contractor should include, but not be limited to, the following:

- All tasks necessary to comply with statutory obligations for tests and inspections of such items as cooling towers, pressure vessels, fire hoses, exit lights, fire pumps, lifts and so on.
- Cyclic maintenance tasks planned at frequencies designed to keep the appearance and performance of the facility at an appropriate standard.
- All maintenance tasks necessary to follow manufacturers' instructions or recommendations. This provision could be modified by the contractor, but only if it could be demonstrated that the recommended schedules were not economic or appropriate.

- Tasks chosen and planned by the contractor to reduce the likelihood of failures and breakdowns and to improve the utilisation of available resources.
- Regular reporting (preferably) through a computer-aided maintenance management system.

Maintenance standards

Obviously, the building and its equipment and services should always be maintained to approved standards, legislation and building codes. There are many standards which will be of relevance. They include both Australian and international standards, as well as occupational health and safety standards. In addition, statutory requirements will set specific requirements for the maintenance of some equipment, ie the treatment of cooling towers and the use of biocides to keep legionella bacteria from developing. Last, there are manufacturer's instructions to be followed, particularly during warranty periods.

In Australia, there are a number of standards which relate to building maintenance. Some of these are listed in the table below, though the list is not exhaustive.

In addition, there is the Building Code of Australia which is a very useful reference tool.[2]

What should be included in the contract?

As part of the maintenance contract a composite picture of the building and its assets needs to be developed. This will include the building's structure and operating systems. The items that should be listed on the maintenance schedule will include the following:

What should be included in the contract?

As part of the maintenance contract, a composite picture of the building and its assets needs to be developed. This will include the building's structure and operating systems. The items that should be listed on the maintenance schedule will include the following:

Building fabric and surrounds

The building's surrounds, including the lawns, gardens, fencing, paths, driveways and perimeter lighting. If the roof is made of tile or slate, an annual inspection should be conducted to ensure that none are cracked or broken and that there is no build up of moss, particularly if the building sits in the shadow of larger buildings.

The contractor should ensure that the gutters and downpipes remain free of leaves, twigs and branches, particularly if there are large trees near the building. Flashings and eaves should be checked from time to time to ensure they have not been affected by water.

TABLE 6 MAINTENANCE STANDARDS

Standard Number	Date	Title
AS1735.10	1986	SAA Lift Code – Tests
AS1851.1–11	1981–1997	Maintenance of Fire Protection Equipment
AS2201.1–5	1986–1992	Intruder Alarm Systems
AS/NZ2293.2	1995	Emergency Evacuation Lighting for Buildings – Inspection and Maintenance
AS/NZ3666.2	1995	Air-handling and Water Systems of Buildings – Microbial Control – Operation and Maintenance
AS3676	1989	Portable Fire Extinguishers – Guide to Servicing

Airconditioning systems

This includes major items of plant, such as air handling units, fans, cooling and heating coils, chillers, boilers, pumps, humidifiers and dehumidifiers, exhaust fans, filters, ductwork, cooling towers and the main control system.

The contractor should also be requested to keep a ready supply of spare parts on site. Having them on hand means there will not be any delays when an existing part needs replacement.

Electrical

There will be a number of distribution boards, switchboards and motor driven equipment located throughout the building.

It is also a good idea for the contractor to keep a stock of fluorescent tubes or light globes on site. Again, this ensures that defective items can readily be replaced.

Fire Protection

Central alarm panel, early warning smoke detection system, emergency warning and intercommunication system, fire suppression system, smoke and heat detectors, hand-held extinguishers, hose reels, fire doors, smoke exhaust system and emergency lights.

Security

Central alarm panel, motion detectors, cameras and surveillance equipment, locks (particularly electronic) and access control systems.

Lifts

Passenger and goods lifts and conveyor belts.

Shelving

If shelving is manually operated, maintenance usually involves the drive systems, eg operating handles. Problems with this type of shelving are generally minor and can be rectified after they occur. If the shelving is electrically operated, the motors which operate the system will require regular maintenance.

The tops of all shelving units should also be programmed for cleaning every six or 12 months. When this is done, any early warning smoke detection systems that may be in the area should be switched off so that they do not react while the work is in progress.

Keeping a maintenance record

As part of the maintenance contract, the contractor should be tasked with preparing detailed reports of all work undertaken, whether preventative or corrective, and ensuring that the maintenance history of all individual building elements and plant items is readily accessible to you. This can easily be done through a computer-aided maintenance management system.

It should be clearly stated in any contract that ownership of all such material rests with you, not the contractor. This is particularly noteworthy if, at the end of a contract, a new company is selected to undertake future work. There are different types of maintenance records and different reasons for keeping them. The first are the basic service reports which list normal services to be performed and have provision for your signature and the contractor which supplied the service. They can serve as a record of all completed work.

They indicate not only that the contractor is meeting obligations but that you are meeting your statutory and other requirements. From the basic service report, it is then possible to prepare more detailed assessments of plant items and identify trends in overall performance and herald any additional work that may be required. These assessments assume much greater importance as the building and plant begin to age.

Large items of plant usually have a set life span and throughout this period there will be times when major overhauls need to be programmed. At certain intervals, say every five or ten years, an item may need a costly maintenance review. By noting that item's maintenance history and performance levels, it can be ascertained if the item is going to warrant this work earlier than anticipated and, hence, whether large amounts of funding will need to be provided sooner than was originally planned. Conversely, it may be possible to delay the work if it can be demonstrated that the item has been performing well.

Basic maintenance which you can undertake

Much of the maintenance work that has been described so far can only be done by trained professionals. There are, however, some tasks that you can perform and, by so doing, be kept directly involved in the whole process. Further, it also helps to reduce your overall maintenance costs.

Simple observation is probably the most obvious way of determining that there is a problem long before it ever becomes a major one. If you develop the habit of making regular inspections throughout the building, both externally and internally, the reward may be twofold – cost savings and avoidance of major difficulties.

The building's exterior

It is an easy matter to walk around the facility from time to time and observe if there are any:
- cracks in the walls, pathways or roads;
- signs of water leaks, spillages or blockages in drains, roofs or gutters; and
- signs of pest infestations.

If there are large trees (especially eucalyptus) near the building, and ideally it is wise not to have large trees in such a location, you can observe if the roots of the trees are causing cracks in the building or leading to the destruction of paths and driveways.

The building's interior

Regular inspections can be made of the storage areas, ensuring that they are effectively sealed against the elements. Staffing and public areas should also be inspected. Observations and discussions with staff will also indicate if there are any potential problems.

Integrated Pest Management

It is, of course, simple logic that purpose-built facilities remain free of unwanted pests such as silverfish, cockroaches, spiders and mice. By keeping them so, you protect both the records for which you are responsible and accountable and help to maintain a healthy working environment for both staff and visitors.[3]

In the past, fumigation was seen as the sole means of eliminating pest infestations. Facilities were often fumigated on a regular basis, eg every six months, even when there was no immediate evidence of pests. Today, it is widely recognised that fumigation is not the sole means of ensuring a pest free environment and, with the dangers present in the fumigants themselves, fumigation should be a last, not the first, resort.

Modern literature[4] now stresses the importance of an overall integrated pest management program as a means to avoiding infestations. The program comprises a number of elements which are set out on page 96.

In accordance with occupational health and safety requirements imposed by many governments, most institutions now have a duty of care to provide a safe working environment for their staff, as well as for visitors to their establishments. Much of what follows, therefore, is your responsibility acting in cooperation with occupational health and safety representatives.

Integrated pest management program

It is recommended that, when planning for a new facility, you should develop and maintain an integrated pest management program as part of this process. At the outset, it is suggested that good building design, coupled with a program of inspections and 'common sense' housekeeping, will go a long way towards ensuring a pest free environment.

Building design

In chapter 2, reference was made to the need for creating a sealed environment in order to maintain stable conditions and help protect the records. The sealed environment has another advantage. It helps keep pest infestations from either developing near, or inside the building.

Attention should also be paid to landscaping. Organic mulching, such as pine chips, should be used with caution as this can be a prime breeding place for pests. It is preferable to use other materials for mulch, or non-organic materials like stones. Likewise, flowering plants are not recommended, at least not adjacent to the building, as they are only likely to attract insects.

Regular inspections for the presence of pests

Regular inspections should be made of the facility, both externally and internally. Such inspections should be conducted at least two or three times each year. Checks should be made for signs of insect or other pest infestations around the perimeter of the building and surrounding grounds, paths and fences.

All roofs, windows and eaves should be inspected to protect the building against entry or nesting by birds.

Leaking taps and pipes (both external and internal) should be attended to as soon as possible to prohibit insect attraction or mould development. In this context, particular attention should be paid to toilets and showers, cleaner's rooms, hot water systems and plant rooms. In short, any areas where there is water.

Regular inspections should also be made of incoming record transfers. If a persistent pest problem is encountered with a particular agency's records this should be brought to the attention of that agency for prompt remedial action.

Good housekeeping

Internal housekeeping measures should also be of a high standard. Obviously, food and drink should never be taken into storage areas. This should not only be brought to the attention of staff but visitors, contractors, or for that matter anyone who accesses the building. Proper receptacles should be provided in the amenities areas for used food and drink containers. These receptacles should be emptied regularly. Foodstuffs should never be left overnight, uncovered or in unsealed containers.

Storage, office and amenities areas should be cleaned on a regular basis. Likewise, external garbage containers should be emptied regularly. Any dead insects, spiders or rodents that are discovered should be removed as quickly as possible.

Deployment of low toxic and non-chemical control measures

Rather than simply resorting to regular fumigation, modern practices now strongly support the use of low toxic and non-chemical measures as a means of firstly identifying the scope of a pest problem and then eliminating it.

There are a number of such measures. First, the deployment of baits and traps. 'Blunder traps', such as Maxforce' or Aqualine', are placed in areas where insects are likely to be found, eg near skirting boards. They contain pheromones, which are chemicals specifically designed to attract insects, such as cockroaches and ants, which may be seeking a mate or a food supply. A pheromone tablet is placed in the centre of the trap and the sticky surface around the tablet catches the insect when it 'blunders' into the trap.

Similarly, baits, such as *Bromokil*™ and *Talon*™, can be used throughout the building in order to poison rodents, eg rats or mice.

Some institutions, even today, rely on cats as a means of keeping their facility free of rodents. As odd as this may sound, it does make sense. Cats have a tendency to present their owners with whatever they have caught and, if there is a problem with rodents, the cat will quickly ensure that you are aware of it.

Traps and baits should be placed strategically throughout the building, particularly in amenities areas and storage areas. They should be inspected regularly and the contents removed to prevent further pest problems. In essence, they serve as the first warning that there actually is a pest problem. Of course, repeated evidence of pests may be indicative of a wider and more significant problem.

The second measure is the use of inhibiting growth regulators (IGRs). These are a group of new chemicals providing long-term residual action which is non-toxic to humans. They target the life cycle of insects by preventing the development of mature insects or ensuring those insects that do survive are sterile. Examples of inhibiting growth regulators include *Roachbomb*™ and *Staricide*™.

Traps, baits and inhibiting growth regulators are cheap and effective means of identifying the extent of a pest problem. They have considerable potential for mass trapping, mating disruption and population monitoring.

Evaluation of results

You should maintain written records of all inspections and findings. These records should be readily accessible and should include dates of inspections, locations or areas, who was present, what was found and what action was subsequently taken.

Application of fumigants

If there is a pest infestation, and all other measures have failed, it may be necessary to apply fumigants.

Prior to fumigating you may wish to consult with other cultural institutions in the same area – such as libraries, museums or art galleries – to determine if they are experiencing the same problems and, if so, what actions they have taken.

It is vital to understand that the use of fumigants should not be undertaken simply as a matter of course nor should it be allowed to become a regular, routine event. It should only be done when there is considered to be a genuine need.

It should never be forgotten that fumigants, no matter what their level of toxicity may be, require extreme care in their handling and use. It is essential when applying fumigants indoors that stringent safeguards are observed to ensure that staff and visitors are not exposed to any risk to their health. The use of fumigants should only be undertaken by experienced and licensed contractors and certainly never by staff.

Suggested procedures for the application of fumigants

Fumigation can take several different forms and means, eg a whole building, floor or perhaps a single room may be sprayed or misted to catch flying insects. Conversely, there may be direct application of a fumigant to skirting boards, cornices and architraves to catch crawling insects.

Only that part of the building that has been shown to actually need it (eg a single room or floor) should be treated.

You should ensure that specifications for the required treatment should be clearly written so that there can be no misunderstanding by the pest control contractor as to what is actually required. The performance of the contractor should also be monitored, evaluated and recorded.

It is essential that you ensure that whichever company is chosen to undertake the application of fumigants is licenced to do so under relevant legislation. The contractor should be asked to provide a list of the chemicals and application methods to be used to achieve the specified goal of eradication of the pests. The contractor should also provide copies of the Material Safety Data Sheets (MSDS) for the chemicals to be used and an outline of all precautionary measures proposed.

The level of toxicity of the chemicals and the dissipation period of the chemical mix (ie how long before it is safe for unprotected staff to return to the work area) should also be clearly stated by the contractor.

Again, all documentation provided by the contractor should be retained by you and be readily accessible if required in the future.

The proposed use of fumigants should be discussed with occupational health and safety representatives and must be brought to the attention of staff and visitors within the affected area.

It is essential that there be foolproof security during the application of fumigants, not only to protect record collections, but more important, to prevent accidental entry to affected areas by staff or visitors which might result in their injury.

> **INFORMATION PROVIDED ON MATERIAL SAFETY DATA SHEETS**
>
> Product name
>
> Other names
>
> Uses
>
> Physical description and properties
>
> Health effects
>
> First aid
>
> Precautions for use
>
> Safe handling information

Common types of fumigants

In Australia, three of the most commonly used fumigants are:

- Dichlorvos or DDVP, an example of which is *Insectigas*™; generally used on building exteriors – walls, paths and surrounds.
- Pyrethrin, an example of which is *Pestigas*™; generally used on building interiors. It is a botanical insecticide and its availability is subject to seasonal variations.
- Deltamethrin, an example of which is *Cislin*™; again used in building interiors. This is a pyrethroid insecticide (a synthetic gas) and is readily available.

The type of chemicals that will actually be used is dependent on the type of pests involved and the size and location (whether internal or external) of the infestation.

In this respect, advice should be sought from the contractor. Once again, the contractor should be licensed and should provide a copy of all Material Safety Data Sheets for all chemicals used. If there is any doubt, you should seek independent advice.

How often should the application of fumigants occur?

There is no set period when the application of fumigants should occur. It is dependent on the need and extent of the pest infestation.

While it is understood that facilities located in tropical areas may have greater difficulty with pest control than non-tropical areas, this does not absolve you from adopting all the low toxic and non-chemical measures outlined above before resorting to fumigation.

When should the application of fumigants occur?

Major applications of fumigants – a whole building or single floor with regular access by staff or visitors – should always take place in the silent hours, ie on Friday nights, weekends or public holidays.

If the entire building is being fumigated, all staff should leave before fumigation commences and not return until at least one hour after the dissipation period has expired. Prior to fumigation, you should inspect the premises to ensure that all staff and visitors have vacated.

Notifying staff prior to the application of fumigants

You must ensure that reasonable notice of the intention to use fumigants is given to all staff or visitors that may be affected. Advance written notice of at least 24 hours is desirable.

The notice should state the part of the building being fumigated, the name of the fumigant being used and the expected period for which the building or area cannot be entered. The notice should also advise that, as all surfaces could become contaminated, food or drink containers should not be left uncovered or exposed and that people may also wish to place computer keyboards, telephones and similar items under cover. Staff notices should be affixed to all entry points. The signs should remain in place until it is safe to enter the area.

Staff should be advised to report any suspect reactions to the fumigant to you or their occupational health and safety representative as soon as they become apparent.

Sufficient notice should also be given so that affected service areas can inform their clients of the potential unavailability of services.

During the period that access is denied to staff, other persons – emergency services or security guards – may need to enter the building or area. They also should be informed of the risks involved. If anyone does enter the area, you and the occupational health and safety officer should be informed.

Some facilities may have security guards based on their premises. Special provision needs to be made for these guards while the fumigation is in progress.

Operation of airconditioning systems during the application of fumigants

Prior to the application of fumigants (particularly spraying and misting), all affected airconditioning systems or zones should be shut down. They should remain switched off for four hours after the spraying has been completed.

It usually takes about two hours for the fumigant to take effect and another two hours for the gas to dissipate. If airconditioning systems remain operational, this will merely have the effect of reducing the impact of the gas.

Those facilities which have early smoke detection devices in place, eg *VESDA*™, should ensure that they have been switched off prior to the application of fumigants, particularly spraying or misting. The sensitivity of these devices is such that the presence of the gas is likely to trigger an alarm.

Procedures following the application of fumigants

Unless there is advice to the contrary, it can be assumed that once fumigation has been completed, and the gas dissipation period has expired, normal commencement of work should proceed.

The contractor should inform you in sufficient time before the anticipated recommencement of airconditioning plant services or occupation of the building by staff if any safety periods have been violated and/or any difficulties have been encountered. You will need to take appropriate action if an adverse report is received.

If you do receive any adverse reports from the contractor or incident reports from staff, then the occupational health and safety officer should be informed. A sufficiently adverse report may prevent the commencement of plant services and the reoccupation of an area by staff.

While occupational health and safety legislation varies across the states and from one country to another, it is generally the case that the accidental spraying of staff, visitors or security guards with fumigants would have to be reported to health agencies.

One last point that is worth considering. Frequent use of fumigants can often lead to the development of resistance on the part of the pests you are trying to eradicate. In turn, you will need more toxic fumigants to cope with these resistant pests. These latter fumigants then pose greater hazards to your staff and the environment. The pests become even more resistant and so the cycle continues. Preventing pest infestations from ever developing is far better than fumigating them afterwards.

Again, it is emphasised that the use of fumigants is a last resort. It should not become a routine event without other options having been considered and evaluated. You should clearly be able to demonstrate that fumigation is the most appropriate course of action.

Disaster Preparedness

So now the building has been built. It is being maintained, the pests are kept at bay and so far all appears to be well. There is, however, one thing remaining; being prepared for a disaster, however remote the chances might seem to be, and having a response plan in readiness.[5]

Reference was made in chapter 3 to the need for having fire and security procedures in place and for all staff to be fully trained and aware of their responsibilities. But in reality it goes further than this. You need to be prepared for any disaster which may befall you. Such preparation involves planning and good procedures which are developed in advance, not simply an ad hoc response to a disaster.

There are basically two types of disasters – those that affect only your institution and those that affect the entire area or city in which you are located. Examples of the first might include a fire, lightning strike, burst water main or a truck ploughing through the wall of your storage area. Examples of the second might include a cyclone, flood or an earthquake.

How you deal with disasters such as these will depend greatly on the preparations you have undertaken beforehand. With the first type of disaster, while the effects to you may be severe you will have external resources available to assist you, eg other cultural institutions, disaster recovery companies and the local emergency services.

With the second type of disaster, it is very much a case of you on your own. If you think you can rely on the emergency services or recovery companies to help you, remember that with a major disaster which affects an entire city the emergency services will, quite rightly, be preoccupied with safety, food and shelter for the general populace. It may be days before they begin to think about repairing the damage to archives and other cultural institutions. So, if your roof has been blown off, your building is partially submerged or the entire structure has been weakened by an earthquake, how will you manage and what will you do? There may be no-one outside of your institution to help.

The floods in Katherine, Northern Territory, in January 1998 have also demonstrated that not only will no-one outside your organisation be able to help, but also you may not be able to rely on your own staff as they may be preoccupied with protecting their personal property.

Preparing for a disaster

The first step is to be prepared and take all the precautions you possibly can. Although a direct hit from a cyclone, lightning or earthquake generally cannot be predicted and certainly cannot be avoided, there are nevertheless a number of things that you can do now.

First, you should conduct regular inspections of your facility, both internally and externally. This will help ensure that good housekeeping practices are taking place and no threats are being posed, for example, from blocked drains and gutters. Such actions will reduce the risk of a local disaster occurring, though of course they will not eliminate the possibility entirely.

Second, you should ensure that your building is as secure as you can possibly make it, with fire and security protective systems in place.

Third, you should create an informal network with other cultural institutions in your city, eg museums, libraries and art galleries, and see what each of you can do to help the others. Ascertain what facilities and equipment each institution has that might be of assistance in an emergency.

Last, identify local companies which can assist in an emergency. Companies may offer a disaster recovery service, or may be able to supply you with materials and storage facilities to help you through the crisis. There are a number of companies in Australia who specialise in providing disaster recovery services, eg:

- BMS Catastrophe (Victoria).
- Munters Water Damage Recovery Services (New South Wales).
- Moisture Control Services (Queensland).

Emergency procedures

You should prepare a set of disaster response procedures and ensure they are available to all staff. The procedures should be easily understood. They should list appropriate names and telephone numbers and show clearly and concisely what is to be done in the first few hours. While the emphasis should be on key information, this should be kept to a minimum. It is generally the case that large disaster plans, with copious notes, will probably never be read, are difficult for people to follow and generally fall out of date more rapidly.

The procedures should always have a review date. All too often it is very easy to issue the procedures and assume that everything will be well. Years may pass and the procedures are never looked at again until the time when they are genuinely needed and by that time are obsolete. So, they should be tested from time to time and reviewed at a preset interval, say every one or two years.

Testing and updating the procedures are equally as important as is the original development. An outdated plan is of no use to anybody and can further complicate matters by (for example) listing obsolete contact persons and phone numbers.

Disaster response committee

As part of the development of your procedures, you should form a Disaster Response Committee which will oversee operations in the event of an emergency.

Who should be on the committee? It should not just consist of people in authority but those who can get to the building quickly, should the emergency occur in the silent hours. Again, you should ensure that the list of members is kept up to date and their addresses and phone numbers remain valid.

It is important that the committee meets regularly to discuss disaster related issues – even if no disaster(s) have occurred. Regular meetings help to keep issues and various responsibilities in focus. Such meetings should be held on set dates and at times fixed well in advance.

Emergency supply kits

You should assemble emergency supply kits and have them located at key points throughout the building and, if possible, outside the building too, in case the kits are damaged by the event. The kits should include brooms, mops, buckets, sponges and cloths, plastic sheeting, garbage bags, torches and batteries, scissors and masking tape. In addition, you could also include protective clothing for your staff, eg gumboots, overalls, gloves and face masks. Such items will help you clean up the mess and will enable you to package damaged, wet or burnt records prior to their repair or other treatment.

The tendency today is to use mobile garbage bins to store these kits. There are several irritations with this. One is that people often think they are simply that – garbage bins – and throw their rubbish in. So the bins need to be clearly identified as emergency supply kits. Second, most bins are quite tall and for the average size person it is not possible to reach in and extract items from them so they have to be tipped over with their contents spilling out over the floor. Last, such kits can be an attractive source of items which your staff might want to borrow for other purposes. So, the contents of each kit need to be inspected on a regular basis. You might also consider applying a seal to the bin which can be broken when the kit is required for an actual disaster.

Vital and valuable records preservation

As part of your disaster preparedness plan, you should identify those records which above all others must be saved in an emergency and those that are perhaps not quite so important. This can often be a daunting task. After all, the view may be that all records are important. Nevertheless, in an emergency situation you will not have the resources to save them all and key decisions should be made in a relative calm atmosphere where they can be discussed and argued rationally.

So, which records will you save? Your own vital records, those which are necessary to the future operation of your institution, or the valuable records in your keeping, ie the ones that are the most highly researched, the oldest ones, the ones that have legal significance? These are not easy decisions, but it is much better to make them now, not delay them till later.

You should also be aware that some record formats are far more vulnerable than others, so that salvage priorities should be set accordingly, eg old film and magnetic tape will only survive immersion for perhaps 24 hours, whereas modern papers (apart from coated papers) may still be retrievable after three or four days of immersion.

Dealing with complacency

You should also be aware of one other key issue. Disaster planning is not just about resources but dealing with complacency and apathy within your own organisation. You may have to react to comments such as:

it can't happen here

but if it does

it will not leave me responsible

but if it does

then there will be help and other resources available.[6]

Obviously, nothing could be further from the truth. Disasters of one kind or another occur regularly and no building is immune from them. There is nothing which can guarantee that your building will not be affected at some stage in the future.

Solid, Safe, Secure: Building Archives Repositories in Australia

Responding to a disaster

Once the disaster has passed, your plan should come into full effect. The building should be secured from any further damage and, when advised by the emergency services that it is safe to do so, the response committee should then enter the facility.

All designated records, and other valuable equipment, should be made ready for salvage. Whatever action the committee takes will, of course, be dependent on the format of the records and the type of damage they have suffered. Generally, damaged material will need to be cleaned, dried, repaired, restored, and undergo more extensive treatment or copying if they are beyond preservation.

Specifically, items may need to be dried, if they have been affected by water, and placed in plastic bags. If they have been burnt they should also be placed in plastic bags. If they are covered in ash, soot, dirt or dust this can generally be removed with gentle brushing.

With most disasters, the main threat to records preservation is the subsequent development of mould which can occur within 48 hours and has been known to take less time. It is a common occurrence as relative humidity levels rise above 60%, and the process can be hastened if the airconditioning system is no longer operating. Once mould takes effect, there is little that can be done, hence when reacting to a disaster, speed is of the essence. One method of preventing mould's continued development is freezing. If there are freezers available and operable, the records should be frozen. Another method is drying using dessicant dehumidifiers.

And remember those companies, listed earlier, which specialise in disaster recovery.

This will be a difficult time for any institution but it can be made worse if there have been no plans and procedures developed beforehand.

Finally, there are the human factors to consider. Remember that a disaster situation can be a traumatic experience. This is particularly the case where there has been death or injury to persons. Such events can significantly delay access to the site and affect the recovery staff. This possibility should not be overlooked in your planning.

Another significant issue which will likely arise is initial enthusiasm by the rescue team turning to depression when (for example) the extent of the disaster is fully appreciated or a belief grows that their efforts are having little or no effect on the situation. The supervisor needs to be alert for these events and to take immediate steps when they appear. In addition, tasks of individual staff members need to be periodically rotated.

In summary, the human aspects are equally significant as the physical steps taken to recover from the situation.

---

1   The section on maintenance has drawn on material produced by Les Cargill of the National Archives when preparing specifications for the first maintenance contract for the Archives' East Burwood repository.
2   Australian Building Codes Board, *Building Code of Australia*, Canberra, 1996.
3   The section on integrated pest management has drawn on documentation prepared by Warwick Peberdy and Elizabeth Donovan of the National Archives.
4   Recent literature on integrated pest management includes: Michelle Berry, *Integrated Pest Management: A Position Paper*, Museum of Victoria, Melbourne, 1993; Thomas A Parker, 'Study on integrated pest management for libraries and archives', UNESCO, Paris, 1988; Alex Roach, 'Current methods in pest control', AICCM (Australian Institute for the Conservation of Cultural Material) Seminar Notes, Canberra, 1993; and *Conservation Online* on the Internet (palimpsest.stanford.edu); the section entitled *Pest Management*.
5   The section on disaster preparedness has drawn on the following publications:
    Stephen Yorke, 'Coping with Disaster: Strategies for the Records Manager', *Informaa Quarterly*, vol. 13, no. 2, 1997, pp. 16–21; Northern Territory Archives Service leaflet, *Disaster Preparedness and Recovery for Records*, Darwin, 1997; Judith Doig, *Disaster Recovery for Archives, Libraries and Records Management Systems in Australia and New Zealand*, Wagga Wagga, 1997; Emergency Management Australia, *Non-stop Service Continuity Management Guidelines for Public Sector Agencies*, Canberra, 1997; and International Council on Archives, Guidelines on Disaster Preparedness and Control in Archives, Paris, 1997 Reference can also be made to Conservation Online on the Internet; the section entitled *Disaster Planning and Response*.
6   Stephen Yorke, *Informaa Quarterly*, vol. 13, no. 2, 1997, p. 17.

Chapter 7
Building in the Tropics

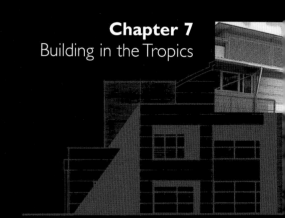

EAST

SOUTH

Operating a repository in a tropical setting will present you with a number of unusual and, in some cases, unique hazards often not found in more temperate settings[1]

First, there are the climatic extremes – temperature and humidity levels – and high levels of rainfall. During a typical wet season in the Northern Territory of Australia it is not uncommon for rainfall levels to exceed 1 800 mm. Given that the average annual rainfall for a non tropical city such as Canberra is only 630 mm the variation between the two is extraordinarily pronounced.

Second, there are the dangers of cyclones, storms and lightning strikes. The Australian cyclone season lasts from November until April. In that time an average of 10 cyclones will form across the north of the country. In addition, cities such as Darwin are prone to extremely violent electrical storms as a result of which major structural or electrical damage can ensue.

Third, there is the ever present risk of pests, such as termites and cockroaches, which can thrive in a tropical setting.

The Site

When selecting a site for your repository the same factors as outlined in chapter 2 apply and we detail here only additional requirements specific for the tropics.

Of course, the prospects of flooding and stormwater damage are even more pronounced in tropical situations. You should never choose a low-lying coastal site. Tidal changes and storm surges, the latter occurring in the aftermath of a cyclone, can result in dramatic rises in sea levels.

It will pay you to make a study of rainfall histories and flood patterns for any sites under active consideration. This task assumes far more relevance in a tropical setting than it would for a non-tropical area.

The site should also be carefully inspected to ascertain if there are termite mounds or nests in the vicinity. Prior to any building activity, it would be wise to ensure that the site has been cleared, with the removal of all dead tree stumps and any other dead wood which might attract termites or other pests.

The Building

At the outset, it can be said that many of the points made in chapter 2 about building fabric apply more strongly in the tropics than they do elsewhere and we refer you to that chapter. Here we concentrate on those points which particularly apply in the tropics.

Building in a tropical setting means that creating a sealed environment with the complete integration of the roof, walls and floor is paramount.

Roofing and guttering are of extreme importance, with roofs pitched sufficiently to ensure rapid removal of rain water.

The building's drainage system should be designed to quickly remove water run-off. Given the huge volumes of water involved this can be a major feat. The photos on page 107 note the circular drainage pits which are placed at regular intervals along the longitudinal sides of the National Archives' facility at Nightcliff, Darwin. The pits are filled with rocks, which reduce the velocity of the water's impact, and collect run-off directly from the building's roof. Located underneath the pits are channels which then transport water away from the property as quickly as possible.

In chapter 2, reference was made to the possible use of vapour barriers in records storage areas as a means of inhibiting moisture penetration from external environments into these areas. There are two ways you can do this. If your building is new, it will be a wise move to have waterproof membranes installed in the walls and below the floors as part of the construction process. But if an existing building is acquired, and problems are experienced, you will need to have a vapour sealant applied and it should cover both sides of all walls which face the storage areas. The process is described shortly under the heading *Case Study 5*.

Environmental Conditions

The tropical environment brings with it excessively high temperatures and humidity levels. Temperatures will constantly remain above 30° Celsius. In the Northern Territory's wet season external humidity levels can remain over 80% for many days in succession. Mould spores are present in the air at all times and basically develop in dark, humid

The National Archives of Australia's Nightcliff (NT) building has 32 cyclone shutters to protect the window glass from flying debris.
Photographs by Ted Ling.

areas when relative humidity levels rise above 60%. The resulting threat from mould and mildew is greater in the tropics than elsewhere and the maintenance of stable environmental conditions is thus paramount. See chapter 3 for details of how to achieve this.

In order to combat these extremes, you need to ensure that your building is sealed against the elements and that, ideally, the storage areas are fully airconditioned. This will help you to keep temperature and humidity levels at acceptable levels and will also promote regular air movement.

If it is not possible to incorporate an airconditioning system in the building's design, or as part of a refit, at the very least there should be good ventilation. Keeping the air moving will reduce the possibility of mould developing, though not eliminate it entirely.

Appendix 3 *Guidelines for the storage of short-term temporary value records (up to 30 years) in the tropics* has been prepared by the National Archives. It provides an overall summary of the conditions necessary for promoting temporary records storage and preservation in a tropical environment. For permanent records storage the same conditions as outlined in Appendix 1 (referred to in chapter 3) apply.

The problem

The National Archives' Darwin facility was constructed in two stages. The first, built in 1975, is used to house permanent value records. The second stage, built in 1991, is used to house temporary value records. The newer stage had vapour barriers included in the walls and floor as part of its construction while the older stage did not.

Problems were experienced in the first stage with high humidity levels, moisture penetration through the walls and mould growth on the external walls of the storage area. This was particularly the case in the pre-monsoon period and during the wet season itself (October to April). The problems only occurred with the first stage, but not the newer stage.

It was proving difficult to maintain constant humidity levels due to a number of leaks in the storage area, ie holes or gaps in the walls and floors. In addition, there were two separate entrances to the area and the doors were an older style, sliding variety which did not create an effective seal when closed.

Last, while the airconditioning in the storage area remained in operation 24 hours a day, part of the problem was due to the fact that of the four walls which surrounded the area, one wall bordered the outside, a second wall bordered the plant room which was not airconditioned and the remaining two walls bordered office and public areas where the airconditioning plant shut down in the silent hours. So, areas outside the storage space often had higher humidity levels than the storage area itself. Thus, condensation could occur on the exterior of these walls and moisture could then migrate through them.

The solution

In essence there were two problems – the loss of environmental conditions and the migration of moisture through the brickwork. What was needed were measures to seal all gaps to help sustain conditions and the application of a vapour barrier to prevent moisture migration.[2]

All gaps in the floor and ceilings were sealed. The bulk of the treatment, however, involved the walls:

External wall (external side only) –

The wall was subjected to a high pressure water wash to remove all surface contamination. A primer coat was then applied (*Dekguard Primer*™) and allowed to dry and cure. Two layers of a protective coating system (*Dekguard Clear*™) were then applied, with a six-hour drying time between coats.

The primer and protective coating system were designed to protect the exposed wall from the effects of rain and general weathering.

Internal walls (both sides) –

All items on the walls, eg wallpaper, racks, posters and other objects were removed. Holes and other blemishes were sealed or repaired.

Exposed shelving in the storage area was covered in plastic sheeting to protect the records while the treatment took place. The walls were then thoroughly brushed and cleaned to remove dirt, dust and any other contaminants.

Two coats of a water-born epoxy (*Emer-Aquashield*™) were then applied with a drying time of two hours between coats. After the second coat had been applied a drying time of 24 hours was allowed and then two coats of a waterproofing membrane (*Emer-Clad*™) were applied with a drying time of two to four hours between coats.

The membrane not only prevents the passage of moisture, it has the added advantage of being elastic. Hence, should there be any minor expansion or contraction in the walls, the membrane should remain intact.

Different colours were used for each membrane layer in order to facilitate overall coverage and to ensure there was an adequate film build.

The old style repository doors were removed. The space left by the smaller of the two doors was bricked up; the brickwork being treated to the same sealant processes as the walls. The larger door was replaced with two inwardly opening doors which maintain a better seal when closed.

The results

Appropriate conditions are maintained inside the storage area and moisture migration and mould development have been halted.

Lessons learned

The major lesson that was learned is the need for an effectively sealed environment in the storage areas to help sustain appropriate conditions for records preservation and the need for vapour barriers to help control moisture migration, particularly in tropical climates.

Integrated Pest Management

Given the propensity of pests and insects to thrive in the tropics, it is imperative that good housekeeping measures be adopted and enforced. The measures outlined in chapter 6, such as regular building inspections, assume greater prominence here. Termites have been mentioned earlier in the chapter and you should look carefully for evidence of pests – nests, webs or droppings – as well as pests themselves.

Protection Against Power Failures and Lightning Strikes

In tropical settings, the power supply can sometimes be erratic and surges, or 'spikes', are not uncommon. Similarly, violent electrical storms can wreak havoc to your electrical supplies, with equipment such as computers and with buildings themselves.

To compensate for the effects of a complete power failure, you may need to consider a reserve power supply in the form of an auxiliary generator. Protection against power surges can be accommodated by means of an uninterrupted power supply unit (or UPS).

Additionally, there is a need to protect your facility against the effects of lightning strikes. Now, there are two issues here. The building itself needs to be protected against a direct hit. To achieve this, the usual method is to install a lightning rod on the roof. The rod contains its own earthing system which is designed to dissipate any potential damage that lightning may cause.

Lightning strikes can, however, occur several hundred metres from your building yet the effects can still be felt. If the strike hits a power line, the surge will travel along the line and into the building's electrical system and, in the worst case scenario, destroy electrical circuit boards, uninterrupted power supplies, back-up systems and their batteries and, of course, computer systems. In a matter of a few seconds your building can be rendered inoperable.

Therefore the facility's electrical systems need protection in the form of a surge diverter. This is a device connected to the main power input and any power surge over a certain level is diverted to ground via the building's earthing system.

Yet you should be aware that lightning strikes can contain power in excess of one million volts and in reality it is extremely difficult to provide foolproof protection against them. At best, you can only hope to reduce the risks or minimise the damage that might be caused.[3]

Cyclones and Storms

Another peril of maintaining a records facility in the tropics is the effects of cyclones.[4] They bring with them excessive rainfall (even by tropical standards) and severe wind velocities. A typical cyclone can release over 250 mm of rain in less than a day and contain winds well in excess of 200 kph.

Cyclones are graded according to their wind velocities on a scale of one to five (with five being the most severe). Cyclone Tracy, which caused catastrophic damage to Darwin on Christmas Day 1974, had wind velocities up to 240 kph recorded. Tracy was a category four cyclone, yet stronger category five cyclones have been known.

Cyclone Rachel which developed off the coast of Darwin in January 1997 managed to bring 311 mm of rain in just one day – a new record – and over 400 mm in little more than 30 hours. Between Cyclone Rachel and Cyclone Phil, one week earlier, Darwin managed to receive over 700 mm of rain in less than 10 days.

To help protect your building from the effects of cyclones a number of features can be provided. First, as stated earlier, it is imperative that the building has adequate rainwater run-off. A pitched roof and a good drainage system will ensure that water is removed from your site as quickly as possible.

If your building has large expanses of glass, it will need protection from wind and airborne missiles. In order to accomplish this, you can install shutters over all glassed areas. The National Archives' Darwin facility has a total of 32 cyclone shutters covering three sides of the building (the fourth side has no windows and does not require shutters). Cyclone shutters are similar to garage roller doors and can be lowered manually when a cyclone is imminent, as is illustrated in the photos of Nightcliff. They are then raised when the danger has passed.

In addition to shutters, your building will also require cyclone dampers which cover all external openings to your mechanical and electrical plant rooms. Dampers look like columns of louvres. Their purpose is to provide you with a means of sealing all openings and thus minimising the effects of wind pressure on the building and its contents. They can be motorised or operated manually.

Each year, prior to the commencement of the cyclone season, the shutters and dampers should be inspected to ensure their ease of operation in the event of an emergency.

During the cyclone season, be sure to make regular inspections of the perimeter of the building and its surrounds to ensure there is nothing that might serve as an airborne missile. Such material – and it can include fallen tree branches and palm fronds – should be promptly removed.

If a cyclone warning is given by the emergency services, the shutters should be lowered, the dampers closed and the airconditioning system shut down. This last point may at first appear contradictory. As stated earlier in this chapter, airconditioning in a tropical setting is seen as imperative for records protection. The difficulty, however, is that during a cyclone there is every possibility that the building may be damaged by wind or lightning strike. If the airconditioning system remains operational, and a fire ensues, the damage can be far more widespread than if the system is shut down.

In this context, if you have an auxiliary generator it should also be disabled to ensure it cannot operate until the danger has passed.

1   This chapter has drawn on a paper entitled *Brief for a Facility to House Records of Short Term Value in a Tropical Environment* which was prepared by Barry Snodgrass of the National Archives. Michel Duchein, *Archive Buildings and Equipment*, Munich, 1988, also discusses issues involved in maintaining an archives building in the tropics; pp. 131–133.

2   The work described in Case Study 5 was compiled with the use of trade literature produced by Fosroc, manufacturer of *Dekguard Primer*™ and *Dekguard Clear*™ and Parbury Technologies Pty Ltd, manufacturer of *Emer-Aquashield*™ and *Emer-Clad*™.

3   Detailed information on lightning protection can be found in Australian Standard 1768-1991 *Lightning Protection*, Sydney, 1991.

4   Educational literature on lightning, storms and cyclones produced by the Bureau of Meteorology was consulted in writing this section.

Chapter 8
The Lone Archivist

EAST EL

SOUTH EL

Even if the facilities at your disposal are less than ideal, you should not despair.

The subjects that have been discussed throughout the previous chapters have been aimed at major facilities which consume large budgets. But the principles espoused can, when scaled down, apply to smaller institutions which have minimal budgets and are operated and maintained by the lone archivist.[1] This chapter is written as a 'stand alone' piece of work, ie it can be read by itself without having to read the previous chapters, although the latter will certainly help. For this reason a number of comments and suggestions made in earlier chapters have been deliberately repeated.

From the outset, it must be recognised that all records, regardless of their physical format, need stable environmental conditions in order to survive. This is a basic fact. It is irrelevant to the records whether or not you have the funds and facilities available to achieve these conditions. Without them, the records are going to deteriorate. So what you have to do is slow this rate of deterioration by whatever means you can.

Even if the facilities at your disposal are less than ideal, you should not despair. Try and approach the problem in an incremental way. And remember, you cannot achieve everything at once.

It is assumed that most lone archivists will be required to use an existing building, rather than a new one, and site selection will therefore represent an assessment of what is immediately available, not acquiring something that is built to a plan. It is further assumed that most lone archivists will only have part – generally a small part – of a building allocated to them rather than the entire facility.

Regardless of the funding that might be available there are still some basic factors to consider and most are the same as for a major facility.

The Site and the Building

The same site selection criteria apply as they would when considering the choice of a multi-million dollar facility. Whatever building is chosen to house your archives, it should be clear of pollutants, clear of tracts of water and close to a main road and public transport. Heavily polluted areas should be avoided as far as possible, even if they might mean cheaper purchase costs or rent. A light industrial area or technology park is preferable.

An assessment should be made of the building's neighbours. You should ascertain if there are hotels or garages or any other nuisance establishments near to the site. Hotels may be a centre for drunks to congregate and subject the facility to vandalism. The fuel tanks in garages pose a danger from explosions.

The ready availability of public transport should be noted. This will, of course, be of interest to both staff and visitors. When considering vehicular transport, it should be noted if there will be sufficient parking for both staff and visitors.

The building and its surrounds should be considered not only in the context of their present suitability but whether they are likely to remain suitable for your needs for the foreseeable future.

The overall functionality of the building should be considered. The manner in which the storage, staffing and public areas will coexist is vital. The ability of your building to cater to present and future work flows should never be taken lightly.

If given the opportunity, and it is recognised that in the real world this will not always occur, you should make a thorough inspection of that part of the building which is being proposed for the archives. This will give you an impression of the quality of the premises; whether they are clean and have been cared for or whether they have been abused and neglected.

Apart from functionality, during the inspection you should look for any signs of possible problems, eg water leaks, stains in the ceiling or floor, streak marks down the walls. There may be musty smells which could indicate rising damp or mildew. The inspection should not be confined to obvious open areas, but should include corners, storerooms and any other 'out of the way' places. If the building has been freshly painted, this could mean something is being hidden and it will pay you to carefully scrutinise such areas.

Ascertain if the building contains any environmental hazards such as asbestos, polychlorinated biphenyls (a chemical compound used in fluorescent light fittings until the mid-1970s) or halon fire protection systems. The first two are dangerous if left in place and all three are costly to have removed.

The building's roof should be pitched, at least 5° or more, and there should be a good drainage system designed to remove water from the building and the property as quickly as possible.

Note the location of the building's loading dock. It should not open directly onto the proposed storage area but neither should it be some distance away, meaning that records have to travel through a maze of corridors. Ease of vehicular access to the dock should also be noted, particularly if there is to be frequent movement of records into and out of the facility. This is not so important if the movement of records is minimal.

A careful inspection should be made for signs of insect pests – dead bodies or droppings – both inside and outside the building. If traps or baits are prevalent the extent of the pest problem should be ascertained. Again, it may be desirable to obtain a pest report.

While it is generally the case that the archives will occupy only a small part of a building, you should be very wary if that part is to be the basement, attic or a similar location. The basement is certainly not the place for an archives but if that is all that is on offer you should attempt to minimise the risks. Ensure that records are not stored below or near pipes, boilers or other items of plant or equipment. If the shelving must be located below pipes, have large covers placed across the top to deflect any water. Keep shelving away from the walls and ensure that all records are housed in shelving and not stored on the floor.

Again, it is imperative that whatever storage areas are to be used, the fabric of these areas should form an effective seal to help you maintain strict environmental controls.

If the walls are made of brick or concrete, the internal sides should be sealed otherwise there is the likelihood that contaminants can be released. Sealing can be achieved with a good quality paint, though you should ensure that the vapours from the paint have dissipated before records are brought into the area.

Likewise the ceilings should be intact; any gaps or holes should be sealed. You should also check above the ceiling to see if there is any form of insulation, which will help minimise the effects of solar radiation in the storage areas.

You may experience problems with moisture penetration, which, unless you are in the tropics, will usually be through the walls. A vapour barrier (a form of sealant) may need to be applied. There are a number of products on the market. For external walls these include Fosroc's *Dekguard Primer*™ and *Dekguard Clear*™. For internal walls there is Parbury Technologies' *Emer-Aquashield*™ and *Emer-Clad*™. These are generally used on a large-scale basis, smaller problems can be rectified by visiting your hardware store and studying the sealants that are on supply.

You should ascertain if the walls and doors surrounding the proposed storage areas are fire rated and, if so, what the fire rating is. Fire ratings are basically the level of time it takes before a fire will burn through or the structure collapses. The longer the rating, the better. It is recommended that a facility should have a two-hour rating, but at the very least it should have a one-hour rating, particularly if your storage areas do not have sprinklers.

It should be noted if there are large expanses of windows or skylights. In effect, there is no place for either in storage areas. Ultraviolet light from sunlight can have a deleterious effect on records preservation and skylights simply mean another roof penetration with the risk of leaks. If there are windows, it is preferable that they be enclosed with insulation and wood panelling, for example. If this is considered too expensive they should be covered with blackout curtains, or similar material.

Any small gaps around the window frames should be sealed. Likewise, gaps around the doorframes leading to the storage areas. Leaks and gaps simply deny you the environmental conditions you are trying to achieve. There are a number of commercial sealants and gap fillers available from hardware stores, including silicone. Dust strips can also be used on doors to seal gaps.

The floor-to-ceiling height ratios should be noted in the context of the intended height of your shelving. Low ceilings may mean smaller shelving rows with an overall reduction in storage capacity. If you intend to use mobile shelving, and the area has sprinklers, in accordance with Australian Standard 2118 *Automatic Fire Sprinkler Systems* you are required to allow 500 mm clearance between the top of the shelving and the sprinkler heads.[2]

The floors should be checked to ensure they are level, which is particularly relevant if mobile shelving is to be used. The ability of the floors to take the weight of fully laden shelving, regardless of whether mobile or static shelving will be used, should also be ascertained. If there is any doubt, you should obtain a structural engineer's report verifying this fact.

Floors should be covered, preferably with vinyl. Carpet is not recommended in storage areas as it generally cannot sustain the wear and tear that vinyl can. It also collects dust and can release small fibres which will simply add to the overall pollution level of the area. Bare concrete floors should be actively discouraged as they also can give off contaminants which will affect both records and people.

The existence of pillars, and possibly internal drainpipes, should also be noted. Pillars can impede the efficient layout of shelving and internal drainpipes carry the threat of water damage if they happen to leak.

Staffing areas

Despite the lone archivist concept, you may have several staff working with you and provision will need to be made for each person. When planning an office layout, remember to allow not only for personal space – desk, chair, computer, visitor's chair, bookcase, filing cabinets – but circulation areas as well. People need to be able to move within their own area, and of course to other areas. It is generally the case that a space of 10 square metres is needed for each person, including circulation spaces.

You should take into account noisy machines, such as photocopiers and printers and, if possible, ensure that they are located where they will not interfere with staff and their work.

The ability of your building to provide for the creature comforts of staff – thermal comfort and lighting – should be considered.[3] Recommended levels are as follows:

temperature   23°–26° Celsius (summer); 20°–24°Celsius (winter)
humidity   40%–60%
overhead lighting   240 lux–400 lux

Ease of access to amenities areas and rest rooms should also be noted. It is preferable that the amenities area be fully separated from office areas, to reduce the risk of food and liquid damage and to avoid the risk of pest infestations. If your facility does not have an amenities area, and you are required to provide one, ensure that it is as far removed from the office area as possible. Use fabric screens, panels or even imitation pot plants to divide the two areas.

Public areas

In the same context, the building's suitability for public use should be scrutinised.

The area will need to cater for the multiple needs of users – people working at tables, using a computer system or a microfilm reader/printer if you have one. They will need space to spread finding aids about them. If they are using plans or drawings they will need a large table. You can, of course, use smaller tables and join them together if a larger, map table is required on an occasional basis.

Remember that many readers now prefer to use their own laptop computers so you will need to ensure you have sufficient power outlets.

Noisy machines, such as microfilm readers, should be screened from general areas so as not to create a nuisance for other readers.

The same thermal comfort conditions and lighting levels will apply as they do for the staffing areas. Be particularly wary of excessive glare from windows and computer screens, as well as noise from the street or other areas of the building. Glare from windows can be countered with good curtains and anti-glare screens can be purchased for most computers. External noise may necessitate double-glazing of your windows or the use of very thick curtains.

It can sometimes be the case that the storage area, staff and public facilities are all in the one room or space, rather than properly partitioned. If this is the situation, the area needs to be effectively segmented to allow all functions to be carried out without impinging on any other. People talking and noisy machines such as photocopiers, printers and microfilm reader/printers can be very distracting so, as much as possible, they should be relegated to out of the way places, such as alcoves or corners. Screens and large, imitation pot plants can be used to help deaden the sounds. Never place real plants in a storage area as the soil is a potential breeding ground for mould and insects.

Environmental Conditions

The maintenance of stable environmental conditions is best achieved by a combination of appropriately sealed storage areas and an airconditioning system.

The extent of your building's airconditioning system, if it has one, should be assessed as should its reliability and its maintenance history. If the building is not airconditioned you should ascertain if it has forced ventilation. If there is no airconditioning or ventilation, as an absolute minimum, ceiling fans will be needed, especially in locations which have high humidity. It is essential that at the very least the air be kept in motion.

If you do have an airconditioning system it needs to be running continuously, even in the silent hours. There is no point switching it off at night or on weekends. While you may save on energy, you will also be hastening the degradation of your records.

What are the right environmental conditions for records preservation? As was stated in chapter 3, there is little general agreement but for paper the optimum temperature range should be between 18° and 20° Celsius and the relative humidity level should be 50%, or as close as possible to this level. For films, photographs and magnetic media the tolerances are less; the lower the temperature the better. Less than 18° Celsius is desirable, with a relative humidity level about 45%.

But regardless of whatever conditions you can achieve, they should always be constant; fluctuations, even minor ones, should be avoided as much as possible.

Now, how do you know you are actually achieving these conditions? You can use hand held probes and recorders which can measure both temperature and relative humidity levels, eg the *Vaisala HM34*™. This is an accurate, though expensive device costing about $500. There are cheaper recorders, eg the *Mini-Max Thermo-Hygrometer*™, which costs less than $100.

What can you do if you are not managing to achieve the desired conditions? Assuming the storage area is as sealed as you can possibly make it, if the temperature levels are outside the optimum range heaters or fans may help, to raise or lower the levels as necessary. If the humidity levels are too high (and, in Australia, rarely will they be too low), use portable dehumidifiers or moisture absorbing crystals such as *Camel Closets*™ or *Damp Rid*™. Dehumidifiers can be purchased or hired. Crystals can be purchased at the supermarket. The latter are cheap and easy to use, though they do need to be replaced fairly regularly.

If your airconditioning system is not purposely engineered to provide the kind of conditions specified here you may find that lower temperature set points may cause unstable humidity levels. If this happens, it is preferable to raise the temperature level, as long as it remains in the low 20s, so that reasonably stable humidity levels can be achieved.

Mould

Mould is a type of fungus. While there are many varieties, it can generally be said that mould spores are particularly attracted to starches and glues found in paper-based products, gelatine emulsions in photographs, leather volumes and 'in-house' dust – which may include residues of all these things, including human skin.

The spores can be carried in the air at all times. If they remain dormant they are not a problem, but when the right conditions occur they become active and, if unchecked, will destroy many record types.

The right conditions for mould growth are a food source (eg paper products and leather bound volumes) and high moisture levels in the air. When relative humidity levels rise above 60%, and remain there, these are the times that mould growth is most prominent.

How do you prevent mould from being a problem in the first place?

First, ensure that you keep the air in the storage areas moving and keep these areas clean. Maintain relative humidity levels below 60%. An airconditioning system comes into its own in this regard. Though if you do have an airconditioner ensure that the filter is cleaned regularly.

Pay close attention to dark corners and damp areas, especially if you are in a basement, which ideally you should not be. The task is to prevent dust and dirt from accumulating. You should ensure that your records are boxed or wrapped in appropriate materials and not simply left sitting on the shelves.

It is important to keep the air moving too. Even if humidity levels are high, good air flow can assist in keeping the air immediately adjacent to record surfaces drier, thus minimising the potential for mould growth. So, if the humidity level is high, and you have no other means of lowering it, try using fans or even natural cross ventilation to establish as much air movement in the area as possible.

How do you know that your records are affected by mould?

The telltale signs that mould is affecting your records are the appearance of brown marks, known as 'foxing', general staining or 'furry' stains and a dank, musty odour.

What do you do if you have mould growth?

Once it is there, it is often the case that the damage cannot be undone. The marks will often remain. But you do need to prevent its further growth.

If the problem is widespread your records may require freezing. This method of treatment can lead to other problems with some types of records and is best done by a professional conservator. Another form of treatment is drying in order to deactivate the spores. Drying can be achieved simply by spreading the records out in a clean, well-ventilated area. To do this they should first be placed in plastic bags and sealed. Once the records have been treated, the cause of the mould, eg leaking pipe or rising damp, should be addressed.

Once the records are thoroughly dry you can then attend to the removal of the mould spores. If only a small number of items have been affected, you can rectify the problem yourself. The treatment should be undertaken outside the storage area. Ensure the area where you are working is well ventilated. Wear latex gloves, a dust coat and a face mask that covers your nose and mouth (at the very least use a paper mask that you can purchase at most hardware stores). Brush the affected surface with a soft bristled brush and gently wipe the spores away. All materials and surfaces used in the cleaning process should either be disposed of or thoroughly cleaned, so that spores do not remain in the area to contaminate other records, or are carried into other areas. You should be very careful not to lean over the object while you are doing this. It is most important that you do not inhale the mould spores as some types can be toxic.[4]

Solid, Safe, Secure: Building Archives Repositories in Australia

Another option is simply to photocopy or microfilm the records and destroy the original copies. However, this may not be appropriate in every case. In reality, it is dependent on the nature and value of the records that have been damaged.

Here we see the damaging effect that mould has on paper.

Lighting and energy management

As stated previously, lighting levels in frequently used staffing and public areas, where concentrated desk type activity is required, should be between 240–400 lux. In record storage areas, where regular access is not required, a level of 80–240 lux is appropriate.[5] Even if the staffing and storage areas are co-located, you should attempt as far as possible to have dual light levels.

To help preserve the records, all light fittings, particularly those in the storage areas, should be fitted with low ultraviolet emitting tubes or ultraviolet filters. Phillips produce two models of the former, eg TLD 36/92 and TLD 36/93. As an example of the latter you can purchase jackets which slide over the tubes. They can be purchased from S and M Supply Company and other suppliers.

Depending on how large the storage areas are, it is wise to have timed lighting installed, though an electrician will be needed to do this. If the area is only small then the main switch should be connected to a timer.

The lighting for the storage and staffing/public areas should be on separate circuits so that the lights in the storage area can be switched off if no-one is working there.

Fire Protection

Fire protection is about the safety of people, the preservation of records and other assets and the building itself, basically in that order.

Protection should be viewed on a number of levels. Obviously, you would like to avoid fires in the first place. But if they do occur, the means should exist to detect them at the earliest opportunity and then they should be rapidly contained and extinguished.

Avoidance and safety

The risk of fire can be minimised with good housekeeping, well-trained staff and up-to-date emergency procedures. Your staff should be trained on what to do in emergencies. It costs little, but their swift reaction may prevent a catastrophe. Evacuation procedures should be tested (and drills held if necessary) at least once each year.

Appropriately maintained equipment (particularly electrical) will go a long way towards reducing the chances of fire. It should be remembered that many fires have their origin with faulty electrical equipment.

Fire exits and emergency lighting should conform to local codes and standards. The *Building Code of Australia* will tell you what they are as applied to your State or Territory.[6] Be sure that all signs and exit lights are clearly visible, particularly if high shelving is being installed. High shelving can often restrict your view of signs and exits.

Fire exits should never be locked on the inside and should be capable of being opened in a single movement, eg 'crash bar' type. They should never have anything placed in front of them, such as stores or furniture that would impede a person's escape. You should also ensure that exits remain clear on the outside of the building – that there are no stores, garbage bins, or even cars, which would restrict movement.

Detection

You should be fully aware and familiar with the building's fire detection system. The nature of the alarm system, number and location of emergency exits and emergency lighting should be determined. Ascertain if the alarm system has a direct telephone line to the fire brigade. Such a line will ensure the brigade is notified automatically whenever there is an alarm. It should also be noted how far the fire brigade is from the building and how long it will take them to reach the facility.

Does your building have a network of smoke and heat detectors? If there are no detectors available, smoke detectors can be purchased from department and hardware stores at a cost of less than $20 and can be easily installed by anyone; an electrician is not required.

Yet it should be recognised that the most potent fire alarm is not always an expensive electronic system; it is the human network. In this context neighbours, if you have them, can readily be used as a 'human fire alarm', at least during business hours.

Containment and suppression

Having detected the fire, there should exist the means of containing it and then extinguishing it. The most effective means of extinguishing a fire is with a sprinkler system or gas flood system. If these are not available, it is desirable that hand held extinguishers be acquired. You can purchase larger, single purpose industrial extinguishers, the type often seen in most buildings. There are two which are the most common – carbon dioxide which are red with a black band and dry chemical, which are red with a white band. Both are suitable for fires involving paper, wood and live electrical equipment.[7]

You should, however, be aware that dry chemical extinguishers can cause major damage if the extinguishing agent comes into direct contact with records. It can be very difficult to remove the agent from the surface of many record types. Very low budget institutions can purchase smaller multi-purpose extinguishers. They cost less than $40 at hardware stores.

There is a tendency to place extinguishers near electrical machines, eg photocopiers, but in reality this is not a wise move. The best place is near major exits or exit routes so that people can reach them quickly and easily. Fire blankets can also be used to extinguish very small fires. Again, they can be purchased at hardware and department stores and are quite cheap.

Of course, only the smallest of fires should ever be tackled. If there is the slightest risk of personal injury the fire should be left to the brigade to extinguish.

Security

The extent of the building's security measures should be ascertained. It also pays to check with the local police station and ascertain if there have been any recent break-ins in the area.

Ideally, you would like to have modern security panels, alarm systems, motion detectors and video surveillance equipment. However, if such measures are beyond your reach there are a few less expensive measures that will be of assistance.

First, all doors should be of good quality and it is preferable that they be solid, rather than hollow core which are often used. Solid doors provide greater security and are more fire resistant. Good quality locks should be installed on all doors and windows too, particularly if there are any in the storage areas. External points of entry, such as the front door and loading bay door, should also have double-keyed deadlocks fitted. All external doors should have their hinges on the inside, ie facing inwards, not the other way. If they face outwards then anyone armed with a screwdriver can remove the bolts and simply pull the door away from its frame.

If expensive video surveillance equipment is out of your reach, it is possible to create a little subterfuge. Camera shells are commercially available which have no mechanism inside. They can be installed in areas where there may be a high risk, eg the reading room. The shells are cheap and quite realistic and have a small flashing red light, thus giving the illusion that they are monitoring someone's activities when in fact they are doing nothing at all. As with fire protection, one of the best forms of security protection is the use of neighbours, or other tenants if the premises are rented. If your institution shares its premises, then each should be encouraged to support the others, creating an informal security network.

There should be good lighting around the foyer areas, loading docks, grounds and parking areas. As far as carparks are concerned there is of course the safety of staff and visitors to consider, particularly at night.

Sensor (ie movement activated) lights can be installed in most areas. They can be purchased in hardware stores and many variety stores and are generally quite cheap though an electrician is usually needed to install them.

Occupational Health and Safety

You should be aware that many things in a building can give off vapours and other contaminants which can affect the health of staff or visitors and can also be harmful to the records you are trying to protect.

Reference has already been made to avoiding bare concrete or brick walls and floors in the storage areas. But there are other things too. Some carpets, curtains and even chairs can release fibres and vapours.

If staff or visitors repeatedly complain of illnesses – sore throats, coughs and colds, running noses – it may be that they are reacting to something in the building. Regular cleaning and maintenance will go a long way towards ensuring the removal of many of these contaminants.

Shelving

Records should never be left uncovered, nor should they be stored on the floor. If possible, shelving should be acquired to accommodate all records. It is preferable that steel shelving be used, not wooden. The latter can give off contaminants and, unless properly treated, is also susceptible to termite infestation and is more likely to burn than is steel shelving.

If you find that you have insufficient shelving to meet your needs and there seems to be no alternative to using the floor, then some type of blocks or pallets should be used so that records are not located directly on the floor. This can make a very big difference should there be a flood in the area. However, you should also be aware that some wooden pallets can release contaminants which may be harmful to your records and can, of course, attract pests.

Shelving components are available from a number of manufacturers. They can be purchased in static or mobile form. Mobile shelving, which is more expensive, means that far greater amounts of materials can be stored over a given space.

If the cost of new shelving is beyond your reach, you can often purchase second hand shelving at government furniture stores. Used shelving should, of course, be thoroughly cleaned prior to use and it may be necessary to have it resprayed if the original paint has been badly damaged. Polyurethane varnishes, eg *Estapol*™, are suitable for this. You should make sure the varnish is thoroughly dried, preferably for at least one week, before using the shelving.

Shelving components are available in a variety of dimensions but the most common are as follows:

height   1 875 mm, 2 175 mm, 2 375 mm and 2 475 mm
width   450 mm, 900 mm
depth   300 mm, 400 mm and 500 mm

Storage Containers and Other Forms of Packaging

All records should be boxed, preferably in archival quality containers. If your budget is such that you cannot afford boxes, then use the cartons that your photocopy paper is supplied in. They are not high quality, but they are sturdy and will provide some protection.

Otherwise, wrap the records in plain paper, not newspaper nor coloured paper.

Another 'last resort' option is to use lidded polystyrene boxes that fruit and vegetables are often packed in. Most supermarkets will give them away. However, these should not be seen as a long-term solution, or used in very large quantities, as they would be a major hazard in the event of a fire.

Boxes

Archival quality containers are now commonly manufactured from fluted board, solid board and polypropylene. They can be purchased commercially, in small quantities, and at fairly reasonable prices. They are available in a large array of sizes to cater for most record formats.

Fluted board containers are made from two layers of paper with a piece of corrugated (or fluted) board in between. These containers are lighter, and generally cheaper, than solid board and are usually just as strong. The fluting gives the containers their strength.

Packaging materials

Standard files and smaller documents should be stored in boxes.[8] Larger documents and certificates should be stored flat, not folded, and placed inside paper folders or plastic jackets.

At this point it is appropriate to include a few comments about using plastics to store records. Plastic is, of course, a very general term and can include many variations. Some plastics include coatings or plasticisers that can cause chemical degradation of records and these should be avoided. The most widely available plastics are:

- PVC (polyvinyl chloride)
- You should not use any packaging materials made from PVC. If the product carries no identification, the easiest way to tell if it contains PVC is if it has a sweetish smell, reminiscent of a new car interior. PVC contains plasticisers which affect the resin binders in photocopiers and laser printer toners, causing them to flow and adhere to other surfaces. In effect, the image transfers from one surface to another. A way to test for PVC is to place the plastic in direct contact with a photocopied image for a few days and put it in a warm place. If the plastic sticks to the image then you know it is PVC.
- Polypropylene
  This is generally a good quality plastic and can be used with relative ease.
- Polyester
  This is generally a good quality plastic and can be used with relative ease. There are different types of polyester; the most appropriate is uncoated polyester (eg *Mylar-D*™).

- Polyethylene

This is a low cost alternative to polypropylene and polyester and is generally safe to use. You should attempt to use only low-density polyethylene (LDPE) resealable storage bags (eg 'zip' bags), the type you can buy at supermarkets. Polyethylene is, however, weaker and floppier than polyester or polypropylene, so it may not be strong enough for large or heavy items.

If you are based in the tropics, and you are storing documents inside plastic jackets, you may need to insert a paperboard sheet into the jacket as well to counter the effects of high humidity levels. If you are planning a project to place records into plastic sleeves try to do this on a day when conditions are dry. You can then be confident that you will not be trapping moisture inside the sleeves as you place records into them.

Photographs should be stored separately in albums. They should not be kept in bundles nor held in boxes or bags. You should use albums of the 'slip in' variety, the type available at supermarkets and department stores. Higher quality albums made from polypropylene can also be purchased for less than $20 and are ideal. In either case, the photographs are held in see through sleeves which protects them and provides ready access to each item. Do not use so called 'magnetic' albums, where photos are held against the page. These albums use plasticisers, which is how the photos are held in position, and can actually damage the photos rather than preserve them.

Like photographs, negatives should be held separately and not grouped in bundles, regardless of whether you have individual negatives or strips. They should be stored in jackets.

If you are storing films, such as Super 8 or 16/35 mm, use polypropylene canisters rather than metal ones. The same applies to the core, or spool, around which the film is wound. Metal canisters and spools generally rust over time and can accelerate chemical degradation of films. If you cannot afford polypropylene canisters use boxes and wrap each film individually.

Maps, drawings and other large items should best be stored flat and placed in plan cabinets or racking. If space allocations, or your budget, preclude this they should be rolled and stored in tubes. They should never be folded as they will crack and tear along the folds. Rolled plans should not be held together with rubber bands as the bands can corrode over time. Depending on the nature and value of each map or plan, you may want to consider using interleaving paper between each item. This will help prevent abrasion, ink transfer and transfer of adhesives between the items. Try to avoid rolling large numbers of plans together as this simply makes retrieval and use more difficult. If possible, fragile items should be supported by rolling them around an inner core, for extra support.

Audio and video cassettes can be stored in boxes.

There are a number of companies throughout Australia which can provide you with archival quality containers and other packaging materials. Some of these companies (and this list is by no means exhaustive) include:

- VisyBoard – archival storage containers made from fluted board.
- Zetta Florence – archival folders and boards.
- S and M Supply Company – general conservation supplies.
- Albox Australia – archival polypropylene containers and jackets for the storage of photographs and documents.
- South and Justice – archival paper, board, boxes and jackets.
- Conservation Resources – archival paper, board, boxes and jackets.

Now a word of warning. The terms 'archival' and 'acid free' are sometimes used fairly liberally. As far as paper is concerned, look for terms such as 'permanent', 'wood free' or 'lignin free'. Or ask if they have passed the photographic activity test (PAT) if you intend to use the material for storing photographs. The PAT test is a form of rapid aging whereby materials are assessed for their long-term suitability for photographic storage. If you are using plastics for photographic storage, look for terms such as 'photo safe' or 'copy safe'.

Maintenance

It is assumed that most of your maintenance will be undertaken by a contractor. If you own the building you should ensure that a maintenance contract is established with a reputable company. The contract should include:

- airconditioning systems;
- fire protection – alarm panels, smoke and heat detectors, extinguishers;
- security – alarm panels, motion detectors, surveillance equipment; and
- electrical systems – switchboards, distribution boards, lighting.

However, there are a number of things which you can do to assist. Storage areas should be kept clean at all times. Regular dusting and vacuuming will help reduce the build up of dirt and dust.

Periodic walks around the building and simple observation will alert you to potential problems. On the building's exterior it will pay to watch for roof leaks, blocked gutters or drains. Internally, look for signs of water marks on the ceilings and walls.

If there is only a small airconditioner, a wall mounted one rather than an entire system, it should be serviced periodically and by a reliable company. Particular attention should be given to the filters; they should be cleaned or replaced as necessary.

Hand held fire extinguishers and hose reels should be checked from time to time. As a guide, industrial strength extinguishers and reels are inspected every six months. Smoke detector batteries should be replaced every 12 months.

Door and window locks should be checked to ensure they are functioning normally.

Integrated Pest Management

The principles of integrated pest management espoused in chapter 6 are readily adaptable to small facilities operated by the lone archivist. Again, the importance of pest control cannot be over emphasised.

The building's surrounds should preferably be kept free of organic mulches as these will often attract termites; inorganic material such as rocks and stones are preferable.

Regular inspections, both internal and external, should be made. Watch for any sign of pest infestations developing, eg dead insects, droppings, webs or nests. Again, pay special attention to dark corners. Look for holes or cracks in gutters or walls and any hollows in retaining walls. Note if there are any dripping taps or pools of water. All of these will encourage pest development.

If there are any holes or gaps in the floors or walls, particularly in the storage areas, they should be sealed. If the gaps are small use silicone. If they are large there are a number of commercial fillers available at hardware stores which should be sufficient.

Good housekeeping and common sense measures will go a long way to keeping the bugs at bay. All incoming transfers should be inspected to ensure that a pest problem is not being introduced to the facility. Ensure that eating and drinking are confined to the amenities area and that rubbish containers are emptied regularly.

If necessary, regular use should be made of:

- blunder (or sticky) traps to catch crawling insects such as cockroaches and ants – *Maxforce*™ or *Aqualine*™;
- baits to poison rodents such as rats and mice – *Bromokil*™ or *Talon*™; and
- inhibiting growth regulators, a new generation of chemicals which prevent the development of mature insects or ensure that those that do survive are sterile – *Roachbomb*™ or *Staricide*™.

And remember that a cat will help eliminate rodents too.

Most of these products are readily available, in some cases at the supermarket, and are generally quite cheap. They are easy to use and dispose of when no longer required. Naturally all products should be handled with care and the manufacturers' instructions strictly followed.

The results of all of the measures you have adopted should be recorded and evaluated. If there is a pest infestation which cannot be resolved by other means, you may have to fumigate. However, fumigation should always be a last resort, and when it is done, stringent safety measures should be vigorously pursued. It should always be undertaken by a licensed contractor. Before fumigating have the contractor advise you what gas will be used and ensure you receive a copy of the *Material Safety Data Sheet* for that gas. The Sheet will inform you what effects the gas has and what safety measures may need to be imposed. Ensure that all staff and visitors are aware that the facility is being fumigated and that access is restricted.

The most commonly used fumigants are *Insectigas*™ (for building exteriors), *Pestigas*™ and *Cislin*™ (for building interiors). You should be aware that *Insectigas*™ contains dichlorvos. This chemical has a long residual life and can have a harmful effect on some record materials. While it can be used on building surfaces, walls and skirtings, it is preferable that it is not used in record storage areas and, certainly, it should never be applied directly onto record surfaces.

Disaster Preparedness

No matter how small the budget, the records under your care are important, or else they would not be there. For this reason disaster preparedness and response plans should be put in place and regularly reviewed. All staff should be aware of what to do in an emergency, whatever form it may take.

You may need to consider purchasing a fire proof safe (they can be bought second hand) as a means of storing key documents, photographic negatives and your accession registers.

Ascertain if there are disaster recovery companies in your area who may be able to assist you in an emergency or if there are other cultural institutions prepared to provide you with assistance and materials.

There are a number of companies which specialise in disaster recovery. They include:
* BMS Catastrophe (Victoria).
* Munters Water Damage Recovery Services (NSW).
* Moisture Control Services (Queensland).

Last, as part of your response plan you should identify which records are the most important to the operation of your organisation. You should be prepared to salvage these records first should the need ever arise. You should also be aware that some record formats will need to be attended to more rapidly than others. For example, computer tapes and colour photographs cannot stand prolonged wetting. Most papers and coated papers (glossies) need prompt treatment, more so than ordinary office bond-type papers.

In the Tropics

There are a number of measures which you can employ to help promote records preservation in the tropics. First, an examination of the region's rainfall history and potential flood problems will be of immediate benefit.

Again, prior to selecting a facility it pays to make a study of the surrounding area and who the neighbours are. Likewise, a walk through the proposed building, noting any signs of water penetration – stains on the ceiling, walls or floor coverings – is a necessity. Note whether the roof and guttering show any signs of rusting and leaking. If the facility is not airconditioned, you should ensure there is adequate ventilation. Ceiling fans will aid in this process, though while they help keep the air moving they will not actually lower temperatures or relative humidity levels.

As has already been stated, in order to reduce the high moisture levels in the air you can use portable dehumidifiers or moisture absorbing crystals.

Small low wattage (50–100 watt) heaters can also be used, though only in very small, confined areas. They too help dry out the moisture from the air. They are not expensive to purchase nor do they consume large amounts of electricity.

The facility should be cleaned and dusted regularly to prevent the build up of dirt and dust. Regular inspections should be made of the facility and its storage areas, particularly in dark spaces. Be extra wary of the possibility of pest infestations, particularly termites which thrive in the tropics.

Other hazards of life in the tropics are power surges, lightning strikes, storms and cyclones. Computers and electrical devices need to be protected against power fluctuations as well as the possibility of lightning strikes. Surge guards are one means of achieving this and can be purchased at hardware stores for less than $20. They provide a limited level of protection, but you should be aware that they will be of no use against a direct lightning strike.

As far as cyclone protection is concerned, all windows and large expanses of glass should have shutters surrounding them which can be closed if need be. If this is not possible, in the event of an emergency cover them with masking tape in the shape of a large diagonal cross from corner to corner. Such crosses will not protect the glass from breakage but will at least reduce the chances of it fragmenting and injuring anyone.

If your system has an airconditioning system, it should be shut down during a cyclone warning. The reason for this is that the building may be damaged by wind, rain or lightning. If the airconditioning system is operating, there is the possibility that the damage could be made worse.

Summary

The following are the basic requirements needed for records preservation as well as providing appropriate conditions for staff and visitors. They assume that you have a very minimal budget.

Building Fabric (see also pp. 29–33, 36–42)
Whatever building is to be provided for records storage the area should be well sealed to assist with the maintenance of stable environmental conditions.

Brick or concrete walls and floors should be sealed to prevent the release of contaminants and to prevent moisture passing through them.

Any gaps around doorframes, window frames and elsewhere should be sealed.

Windows or skylights in the storage areas should be avoided if possible; if they are already there they should be covered.

The building should have a pitched roof and a good drainage system.

The building should be free of environmental hazards, such as asbestos and polychlorinated biphenyls.

Environmental Conditions (see also pp. 44–48)
The aim should be to establish a temperature range of 18°–20° Celsius and relative humidity of 50% for paper storage and less than 18° Celsius and 45% relative humidity for black and white film and magnetic media.

Whatever conditions are achieved they should remain constant at all times and should be monitored.

Ceiling fans should be used to keep the air moving if there is no airconditioning system.

Heaters, fans, dehumidifiers and moisture absorbing crystals should be used whenever conditions stray outside the nominated parameters.

Lighting (see also pp. 52–55)
The lighting levels in the staffing and public areas should be between 240 lux and 400 lux. For the storage areas they should be between 80 lux and 240 lux, depending on the level of usage.

Light fittings in the storage areas should be fitted with low ultraviolet emitting lights or have ultraviolet filters placed over them.

Fire Protection (see also pp. 55–61)

Whatever fire safety systems are available in the building they should be known and understood by all staff. All exits should be clearly identified and emergency lighting should be kept in working order. At the very least, storage areas should be fitted with smoke detectors. A supply of hand held extinguishers should be available and staff should know how to use them.

Security (see also pp. 61–63)

Solid doors with double-keyed deadlocks should be used, particularly for the storage areas.

Door hinges should face inwards.

Locks should be placed on all windows.

Records Storage (see also pp. 71–75)

All records should be held in containers, preferably archival containers, and should be stored in shelving, not on the floor.

Staffing and Public Areas (see also pp. 75–78)

These areas should be designed to be functional and to provide for the creature comforts of the people using them.

Maintenance (see also pp. 92–100)

A program of regular maintenance should be developed. At the very least, the facility should be dusted and cleaned regularly. A program of regular walking inspections, both inside and outside the facility, should be implemented.

Integrated Pest Management (see also pp. 95–100)

A program of good housekeeping and cleaning, regular inspections and monitoring for pests should be implemented.

Disaster Preparedness (see also pp. 100–103)

Disaster preparedness and response plans should be developed.

Further Advice

Remember that you are not alone. You have access to other sources of expertise, including the Internet. Many Australian and international archival institutions have websites. Most can be found on the Archives of Australia website (www.archivenet.gov.au).

The National Archives has produced a series of preservation leaflets under the banner *Archives Advice*. A number of these are of special relevance to the lone archivist, including:

1. Protecting and handling paper files
4. Protecting and handling gramophone discs
5. Protecting and handling magnetic media
7. Protecting and handling photographs
10. Caring for your family archive
11. Archival quality packaging.

They are all available on the National Archives website (www.naa.gov.au).

Another notable Internet reference source is Conservation Online operated by Stanford University (palimpsest.stanford.edu).

1   In addition to this chapter, other handy hints for the lone archivist can be found in Leo J Ansell's, *The Small Archive's Companion*, Toowoomba, 1987 and the journal *Practical Archivist*, produced by Joanne Birkl and Anne Cooke.

2   Australian Standard 2118.1-1995, *Automatic fire sprinkler systems*, Sydney, 1995, p. 56.

3   Comcare Australia, *Officewise: A guide to health and safety in the office*, OHS Book 1, Canberra, 1996. This publication contains much useful information on setting up and maintaining a wide range of conditions in office areas. An earlier publication by Comcare Australia, *Airconditioning and thermal comfort in Australian Public Service offices*, Canberra, 1994, is also quite useful.

4   For further information on mould you should consult Northeast Document Conservation Center's Technical Leaflet *Protecting Books and Paper against Mold*, Andover, 1997 which is available on the Internet (www.nedcc.org/mold.htm).

5   Australian Standard 1680.1-1990 *Interior lighting Part 1: general principles and recommendations*, Sydney, 1990, p. 16.

6   Australian Building Codes Board, *Building Code of Australia*, Canberra, 1996.

7   Commonwealth Fire Board Fire Safety Circular 96, *Portable Fire Extinguishers: Suitability for Different Kinds of Small Fires*, 1995.

8   The description of packaging materials and plastics was drawn from notes provided by Kylie Scroope, Assistant Director Preservation, of the National Archives.

Chapter 9
Summary

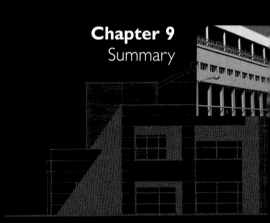

EAST

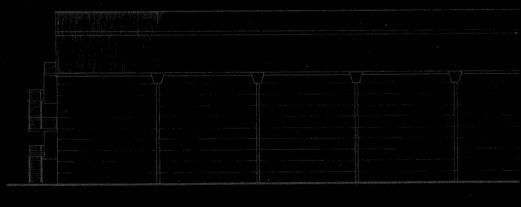

SOUTH

If proper consideration is given to the selection of a site and the design and construction of your building, you will be well on the way to achieving what would be regarded as the ideal archival facility.

What follows is a simple checklist which reiterates many of the points already stated in this book. The checklist highlights issues relevant from the very early days of the project, through the design and construction stages and finally, the day-to-day operation of your building.

But these issues do not apply just to you. They apply to the architect who is designing the building, to the engineers and the builder too. And for that matter they apply to the people who are going to work in the building and care for it afterwards.

Site Selection

Do not choose a site (at least if it can be helped) that is:
- near heavy industry or other pollutants;
- on a flood plain or near other tracts of water; and
- below a major flight path.

But do choose a site that is:
- near a freeway and public transport connecting the facility with the city; and
- capable of future expansion if needed.

Building Design

Design the building so that:
- it is sited to make the maximum use of solar light and radiation for the occupied areas and minimum use for the storage areas;
- it blends in with its surrounds and makes the most of its location, rather than stand as a stark reminder of its presence;
- it is built from low maintenance materials;
- it helps to create a fully sealed environment using the walls, floor and roof in an integrated form;
- the building materials assist in maintaining a pest free environment;
- it provides sufficient records storage capacity for a minimum ten year period before expansion is needed; and
- it is capable of future expansion if needed, either upwards or outwards.

Advise the architect to:
- keep pillars to a minimum in the storage areas; and
- avoid the use of 'dog-leg' corners in and around the storage areas.

Do not have:
- walls without vapour barriers, particularly in locations with high humidity levels;
- walls with inadequate fire ratings;
- with inadequate fire ratings;
- a building with a flat roof or box gutters;
- a roof with multiple penetrations; they should be kept to an absolute minimum;
- internal drainage pipes in the storage areas;
- windows in the storage areas;
- skylights in the storage areas;
- floors without vapour barriers, particularly in locations with high humidity levels;
- floors in the storage areas without coverings; at the very least they should be sealed;
- floors with insufficient loadings to take the weight of records to be held on them;
- insufficient floor-to-ceiling height levels; the precise height of shelving, bases and tracks should be calculated and, in addition, clearance for fire suppression systems should be taken into account;

- loading docks which open directly onto storage areas; airlocks should be used;
- loading docks with shallow entrances so that large vehicles cannot pass through them;
- loading docks with driveways that slope downwards towards the building and inadequate drainage;
- large items of plant inside the building with no way to get them out at a later stage;
- the building's principal air intakes in the car park, or facing the prevailing winds or near other pollutants; and
- large trees near the building, particularly the eucalyptus variety.

Internal Environmental Conditions

Do:
- strive to maintain constant temperature and relative humidity levels for each different record format; for paper the range should be between 18°–20° Celsius and 50%; for black and white film and magnetic media the range should be less;
- provide a regular supply of clean, filtered air that is kept moving throughout the building;
- monitor the conditions being achieved in all storage areas; and
- ensure that there is no leakage of conditions from the storage areas due to poorly sealed doors or frames.

Energy Management and Lighting

Do:
- study energy suppliers' tariffs and ensure that the building makes use of the most economic tariffs available;
- provide a lighting system that divides the building into zones and uses time switches;
- use long life light fittings capable of emitting minimal ultraviolet light, or install filters over the fittings;
- use diffusers over your light fittings to reduce the glare and spread the light more evenly;
- remember to take into account high mobile shelving in the storage areas when determining the placement of light fittings on a master plan, to ensure there are no 'dark spots'; and
- provide an emergency power supply for the building that has the capacity to cater for all services when called upon to do so.

Fire Protection

Do:
- provide a comprehensive fire protection system for the building;
- include a fire suppressant (sprinklers or gas) as part of this system;
- undertake formal fire surveys every three years;
- have staff undertake safety checks and inspections at regular intervals; and
- ensure all staff are trained in fire safety procedures.

Security

Do:
- provide a comprehensive security protection system for the building;
- undertake formal security surveys and threat assessments at regular intervals; and
- ensure all staff are trained to appreciate the need for appropriate security measures.

Staff and Public Facilities

Do:

- create functional, and aesthetically pleasing areas, and remember occupational health and safety issues when planning these areas;
- make the maximum use of natural lighting;
- remember to take into account thermal comfort, lighting and noise levels when planning these areas; and
- remember to provide facilities for disabled persons, both staff and visitors.

Maintenance

Do, from the moment of the building's completion:

- initiate a comprehensive maintenance program;
- keep a written record of all maintenance work, problems that have been encountered and remedial work; and
- as part of this program, remember to develop a pattern of regular 'walk around' inspections which may indicate the early appearance of more serious problems.

Integrated Pest Management

Do, from the moment of the building's completion:

- adopt an integrated pest management program and monitor carefully; and
- as part of this program, remember to develop a pattern of regular 'walk around' inspections which may indicate the early appearance of more serious problems

Do not:

- fumigate the building unless it is absolutely necessary (not as a routine event) and do ensure that stringent safeguards are imposed whenever fumigation is undertaken.

Disaster Preparedness

Do, from the moment of the building's completion:

- develop disaster preparedness and response plans; and
- test and review these plans at regular intervals.

As Constructed Drawings and Manuals

Do :

- ensure that a complete set of drawings and operational manuals is received at the building's completion and that they are kept up-to-date and remain readily accessible.

Conclusion

It is recognised that in the real world it may not be possible to achieve all that is sought. Political interference may come to the fore during the site selection process and budgetary restrictions may limit overall planning.

Nevertheless, if you are given reasonable freedom and adequate finance, the factors outlined above are what you should strive for if the end product is able to meet all the demands placed upon it.

Select Bibliography

This bibliography does not pretend to be exhaustive. It does, however, concentrate on a wide array of sources published over the past 50 years. It also gives prominence to English publications and, further, gives emphasis to Australian publications which are generally omitted from American and European bibliographies.

Acland, Glenda I	'Queensland State Archives', *Archives and Manuscripts*, vol. 21, no. 1, 1993, pp. 150–154 'Review of *The Records Continuum*', *Archives and Manuscripts*, vol. 23, no. 1, 1995, pp. 100–107
Ansell, Leo J	*The Small Archive's Companion*, Church Archivists Society, Toowoomba, 1987
Australian Building Codes Board	*Building Code of Australia*, Canberra, 1996
Ballantyne, Derek	'Planning new facilities - building from experience', *The Archivist*, vol. 19, no. 2, 1992, pp. 18–19 'Conservation areas in the new building of the National Archives of Canada', *Janus*, 1995.2, pp. 94–97
Bell, Lionel	'The Archivist and his accommodation', *Archivaria*, 8, 1979, pp. 83–90 'Archival accommodation in the United Kingdom', *Journal of the Society of Archivists*, vol. 6, no. 6, 1980, pp. 345–364
Berry, Michelle	*Integrated Pest Management: A Position Paper*, Museum of Victoria, Melbourne, 1993
Bladen, F M	'Report on European archives', *Parliamentary Papers*, vol. II, 1903, pp. 993–997
British Standard Institution Standard 5454	*Recommendations for storage and exhibition of archival documents*, London, 1977 and 1989
Buchmann, Wolf	'Planning an archive building: the cooperation between architect and archivist', *Mitteilungen des Oesterreichischen Staatarchivs, Festschrift fuer Rolf Neck*, 1986, volume 39, pages 202–217 *Preservation: Buildings and Equipment*, paper presented to the 5th European Conference on Archives, Barcelona, May 1997
Christoffersen, Lars D	*Zephyr Passive Climate Controlled Repositories Storage Facilities for Museum, Archive and Library Purposes*, Lund University, Lund, 1995
Carrier Corporation	*Basic Concepts of Air-conditioning Systems*, New York, 1982 *Central Station Air Handling Equipment*, New York, 1984
Comcare Australia	*Officewise: A guide to health and safety in the office*, OHS Book 1, Canberra, 1996 *Air-conditioning and Thermal Comfort in Australian Public Service Offices*, Canberra, 1994
Commonwealth Fire Board (of Australia)	*Circulars*, various numbers and publication dates

Cross, John

'The planning and progress of the new archives building in New South Wales', *Proceedings of the 17th Biennial Conference of the Library Association of Australia* held in Perth, August 1973, pp. 217–234

Doig, Judith

Disaster Recovery for Archives, Libraries and Records Management Systems in Australia and New Zealand, Charles Sturt University, Wagga Wagga, 1997

Druzik, James and Banks, Paul

'Appropriate standards for the indoor environment', *Conservation Administration News*, 62/63, 1995, pp. 2-9

Duchein, Michel

Archive Buildings and Equipment, KG Saur, Munich, 1988

Dunn, F I

'Security', *Society of Archivists Best Practice Guideline* 2, London, 1984

Emergency Management Australia

Non-stop Service Continuity Management Guidelines for Public Sector Agencies, Canberra, 1997

Giese, Diana

'Preservation in the Tropics', *National Library of Australia News*, vol. V, no. 8, 1995, pp. 12–15

Gondos, Victor

'Collaboration between archivists and architects in planning archives buildings', *Buildings and Equipment for Archives*, Bulletin of the National Archives, no. 6, Washington, 1944, pp. 9–21
'American archival architecture', *Bulletin of the American Institute of Architects*, vol. 1, no. 4, 1947, pp. 27–32
'Archival buildings – programming and planning', *American Archivist*, vol. 27, no. 4, 1964, pp. 467–483
Archives and Records Center Buildings, Washington, 1970

Hammond, Jay

'Adaptive reuse of old buildings for archives', *American Archivist*, vol. 45, no. 1, 1982, pp. 11–18

Hoechst Celanese Polyester Intermediaries

Ethylene Oxide User's Guide, located on the Internet (www.hcc.com/eo/contents.htm), 1995

Iacovino, Livia

'Australian Archives Victorian Office East Burwood Repository', *Archives and Manuscripts*, vol. 22, no. 2, 1994, pp. 442–447

International Council on Archives

'Proceedings of the 1989 meeting of ICA/CBQ on the adaptation of existing buildings for archival needs', *Janus*, 1992.1, pp. 49–86
'Proceedings of the 1990 meeting of ICA/CBQ on security in archive buildings', *Janus*, 1992.1, pp. 87–123
Guidelines on Disaster Preparedness and Control in Archives, Paris, 1997
'Modern Buildings of National Archives', *Archivum*, ICA vol. XXXI, Munich, 1986

International Standards Organisation

ISO/TC46/SC10 Information and Documentation/Physical keeping of Documents DIS 11799: 1998 *Information and Documentation - Storage Requirements for Archive and Library Materials*, Copenhagen, 1998

Johnson, A K

A Guide for the Selection and Development of Local Government Records Storage Facilities, NAGARA Local Government Records Technical Publication Series, No. 1, 1990

Kennedy, Jean

'Norfolk Record Office fire: an initial report', *Journal of the Society of Archivists*, vol. 16, no. 1, 1995, pp. 3–6

Beasley Kepley, Brenda	'Archives: accessibility for the disabled', *American Archivist*, vol. 46, no. 1, 1983, pp. 42–51
Kitching, Christopher	*Archive Buildings in the United Kingdom 1977–1992*, London, 1993
Klasinc, Peter Pavel	'Archives on the move', *Atlanti*, 4, 1994, pp. 113–117 'Archival functions and the adaptation of existing buildings for archival needs', *Atlanti*, 5, 1995, pp. 101–105
Lamb, W Kaye	*Development of a National Archives*, Parliamentary Paper no. 16 of 1973
Ling, Ted	'Silver linings: purpose-built repositories – the last 25 years', *Archives and Manuscripts*, vol. 22, no. 2, 1994, pp. 360–383 'Repository Design and Management', paper presented to the Conference of the Australian Society of Archivists, Alice Springs, May 1996
McKay, Roger S	'Fine water spray – a halon replacement option', *Fire Surveyor*, June 1993, pp. 16–20
Metcalf, Keyes D	*Planning Academic and Research Library Buildings*, New York, 1965
National Archives	*Functional Brief for the Construction of a Purpose Built Repository for Australian Archives, Victoria*, Melbourne, 1991 *Guidelines for Environmental Conditions and Safety and Protection Levels for Storage*, Charts 1–3, Canberra, 1997 *Archives Advice*, various numbers, Canberra, 1997 *Guidelines for Mobile Shelving for Archives, Libraries and Musuems*, Canberra 1997
National Fire Protection Association USA	*Manual for Fire Protection for Archives and Records Centers*, NFPA 232AM, Quincy, Massachusetts, 1986
Neirinck, Danielle	'The role of the Technical Service of the *Direction des Archives* in the construction of archival buildings in France', *American Archivist*, vol. 53, no. 1, 1990, pp. 140–146
Northeast Document Conservation Center	Technical Leaflet *Protecting Books and Paper against Mold*, Massachusetts, USA, 1997
Northern Territory Archives Service	*Disaster Preparedness and Recovery for Records*, Darwin, 1997
Nugent, Ann	'A Thinking Building', *National Library of Australia News*, vol. 4, no. 8, 1994, pp. 17–21
Pacifico, Michele F	'The National Archives at College Park', *Government Information Quarterly*, vol. 13, no. 2, 1996. pp. 117–131
Padfield, Tim	'Climate control in libraries and archives', paper given to the Preservation of Library Materials Proceedings Conference held at the National Library of Vienna, April 1986, New York 1987, volume 2, pp. 124–138
Parker, Thomas	*A Study on Integrated Pest Management for Libraries and Archives*, UNESCO, Paris, 1988

Parliamentary Standing Committee on Public Works	*Report relating to the proposed construction of an Archives Repository at Villawood, New South Wales*, Canberra, 1970 *Report relating to the Construction of a New Permanent Repository for Australian Archives at East Burwood, Victoria*, Canberra, 1992
Petherbridge, Guy	'Environmental and housing considerations for the preservation of modern records – a guide for the records manager', *Proceedings of the 8th National Convention of the Records Management Association of Australia*, Darwin, 1991, pp. 122–173
Public Record Office of Victoria	*Draft Functional Brief*, Melbourne, 1997
Richards, Kenneth W	'New Jersey's new archival facilities', *American Archivist*, vol. 27, no. 4, 1964, pp. 485–490
Ritzenthaler, Mary Lynn	*Archives and Manuscripts Conservation: A Manual on Physical Care and Management*, Society of American Archivists, Chicago, 1983
Roach, Alex	*Current Methods in Pest Control*, Australian Institute for the Conservation of Cultural Material seminar notes, Canberra, 1993
Rowoldt, Sandra	'The greening of archive buildings: natural air-conditioning in the Southern African context', *Janus*, 1993.2, pp. 36–41
Saclier, Michael	'Buildings for archives and public records', *Proceedings of the 16th Biennial Conference of the Library Association of Australia* held in Sydney, August 1971, pp. 239–249
Schellenberg, T R	'Modern archival buildings', *Archivum*, vol. VI, 1956, pp. 88–92
Schoenberner, Robert A	'What the architect needs to know about archives', *American Archivist*, vol. 27, no. 4, 1964, pp. 491–493
Sharman, Robert	'New building for old. The transmigration of the Queensland State Archives', *Archives and Manuscripts*, vol. 3, no. 7, 1968, pp. 25–35
Shepilova, Irena G and Thomas, Adrienne G	*Main principles of fire protection in libraries and archives: A RAMP study*, Paris, 1992
Simon, Louis A	'Some observations on planning archives buildings', 'Buildings and Equipment for Archives', *Bulletin of the National Archives*, no. 6, Washington, 1944, pp. 3–8
Smith, Brian S	'A standard for record repositories', *Journal of the Society of Archivists*, vol. 12, no. 2, 1991, pp. 114–122
Smith, David P	'Water mist fire suppression', *Fire Safety Engineering*, vol. 2, no. 2, 1995, pp. 10–15
Smith, Wilfred	*Archives in New Zealand*, Archives and Records Association of New Zealand, Wellington, 1978
Standards Australia,	• AS1680.1-1990, *Interior Lighting Part 1: General Principles and Recommendations*, Sydney, 1990 • AS2118.1-1995, *Automatic Fire Sprinkler Systems*, Sydney, 1995
Stanford University,	*Conservation Online* on the Internet (www.palimpsest.stanford.edu/)
Stevens, Craig	*Air-conditioning in the Australian Archives*, Sydney, 1996

Thomas, David	'Archive buildings: international comparisons', *Journal of the Society of Archivists*, vol. 9, no. 1, 1988, pp. 38–44
Thomson, Garry	*The Museum Environment*, Butterworths, London, 1977 and 1986
den Teuling, Arnold	'Environmental conditions for the storage of archival materials', *Janus*, 1996.2, pp. 110–118
Wallot, Jean-Pierre	'Message from the National Archivist of Canada', *The Archivist*, number 114, 1997, pp. 2–4
Warden, Vicki	'The New Queensland State Archives building', paper presented to the Conference of the Australian Society of Archivists, Townsville, May 1994, pp. 48–55
Wilson, William K	*Environmental Guidelines for the Storage of Paper Records, National Information Standards Organization*, TR01-1995, Bethesda, 1995
Winter, Georg	'Gedanken uber einen Archiv-Neubau', *Archivum*, vol. VI, 1956, pp. 93–99
Wright, N O	'What the construction company needs to know about archives', *American Archivist*, vol. 27, no. 4, 1964, pp. 467–484
Yorke, Stephen	'Coping with disaster: strategies for the records manager', *Informaa Quarterly*, vol. 13, no. 2, 1997, pp. 16–21

APPENDIX 1

GUIDELINES FOR ENVIRONMENTAL CONDITIONS AND SAFETY AND PROTECTION LEVELS FOR STORAGE:
PERMANENT AND LONG-TERM TEMPORARY VALUE RECORDS (30 YEARS AND OVER)

FORMAT	ENVIRONMENTAL CONDITIONS			SAFETY AND PROTECTION				PROTECTIVE PACKAGING
	TEMP/RH	AIR QUALITY	LIGHTING	FIRE	SECURITY	HOUSING	CONTAINERS	
Paper (a) files, cards, volumes, computer printout and other papers	20°C and 50%RH; Difference between maximum and minimum values shall be ±2°C and ±5%RH	• filtered to exclude: dust and other particles; acidic and oxidising gases • well ventilated	• UV filtered fluorescent lighting • timer controlled switches	• heat/smoke detection • fire alarms • sprinkler system • extinguishers	• 24 hour physical or electronic surveillance • alarm systems • controlled access	• powder coated or baked enamel metal shelves	• archival quality acid-free boxes	• archival quality acid-free file covers, folders or envelopes
Paper (b) maps, plans, charts	• as above	• as above	• as above	• as above	• as above	• powder coated or baked enamel metal shelves or plan cabinets • flat storage	• archival quality acid-free folders or containers	• archival quality acid-free enclosures or interleaving
Photographic media (a) black and white, sheet film, cine film, X-rays, microforms, glass plate photos	<18°C and 35% RH	• as above • NB degrading cellulose acetate or nitrate films must be isolated from other records	• as above	• VESDA™ (very early smoke detection apparatus) • fire alarms • extinguishers • gas flooding or sprinkler system	• as above	• as above • NB glass plates require stationary shelving and vertical storage	• archival quality acid-free containers or boxes • glass plates require additional shock protection	• archival quality acid-free sleeves, envelopes, enclosures or canisters
Photographic media (b) colour, sheet film, cine film	• maximum stability required • <5°C • 35%RH±5%	• as above • NB records must be acclimatised before and after cold storage	• as above	• as above	• as above	• as above • (may be in a freezer/refrigerator)	• as above	• as above • frozen material must be in sealed vacuum packages
Magnetic media computer tapes and disks, video tapes, audio tapes, magneto-optical disks	• maximum stability required • 18°C ±2°C • 35%RH±5%	• as above	• as above	• as above	• as above	• non-magnetisable shelving	• non-magnetisable, archival quality sealed containers, cassettes cases or sleeves	
Optical media compact and mini disks, laser disks	• as above	• as above	• as above	• as above	• as above	• powder coated or baked enamel metal shelves	• archival quality acid-free containers or boxes	• archival quality acid-free envelopes or enclosures
Miscellaneous gramophone disks, models, objects, mixed media items	• maximum stability required • 20°C ±2°C • 50% RH±5%	• as above	• as above	• as for paper records	• as above	• as above • stationary shelving • gramophone disks require vertical storage	• as above	• archival quality acid-free enclosures or wrapping

Published as part of A54390 *Records Management Part 6: Storage* by Standards Australia

APPENDIX 2

GUIDELINES FOR ENVIRONMENTAL CONDITIONS AND SAFETY AND PROTECTION LEVELS FOR STORAGE:

SHORT-TERM TEMPORARY VALUE RECORDS (UP TO 30 YEARS)

| FORMAT | ENVIRONMENTAL CONDITIONS | | | | SAFETY AND PROTECTION | | | | PROTECTIVE |
	TEMP/RH	AIR QUALITY	LIGHTING	FIRE	SECURITY	HOUSING	CONTAINERS	PACKAGING
Paper (a) files cards volumes computer printout and other papers	• temperature not exceeding 27°C • relative humidity not exceeding 60%	• well ventilated	• ambient light	• heat/smoke detection • fire alarms • sprinkler system • extinguishers	• intruder resistant area • controlled access	• coated metal shelves	• robust, clean containers	• file covers, folders or envelopes
Paper (b) maps plans charts	• as above	• as above	• as above	• as above	• as above	• coated metal shelves or plan cabinets • rolled or vertical storage is acceptable	• robust, clean folders or containers	• individual enclosures not required
Photographic media **black and white** **or colour** sheet film cine film X-rays microforms prints	• 20°C ± 2°C • 50% RH ± 5%	• as above	• as above	• as above	• as above	• coated metal shelves	• robust, clean containers	• clean folders or enclosures
Magnetic media computer tapes and disks video tapes audio tapes magneto-optical disks	• as above	• as above	• as above	• as above	• as above	• non-magnetisable shelving	• non-magnetisable, sealed containers, cassettes cases or sleeves	
Optical media compact and mini disks laser disks	• as above	• as above	• as above	• as above	• as above	• coated metal shelves	• clean, robust containers or boxes	• clean envelopes or enclosures
Miscellaneous gramophone disks models objects mixed media items	• temperature not exceeding 27°C • relative humidity not exceeding 60%	• as above	• as above	• as above	• as above	• as above	• as above	• clean enclosures or wrapping

APPENDIX 3

GUIDELINES FOR ENVIRONMENTAL CONDITIONS AND SAFETY AND PROTECTION LEVELS FOR STORAGE:

SHORT-TERM TEMPORARY VALUE RECORDS (UP TO 30 YEARS) IN THE TROPICS

FORMAT	ENVIRONMENTAL CONDITIONS			SAFETY AND PROTECTION				PROTECTIVE PACKAGING
	TEMP/RH	AIR QUALITY	LIGHTING	FIRE	SECURITY	HOUSING	BUILDING	
Paper (a) files, cards, volumes, computer printout and other papers	• temperature not exceeding 27°C • relative humidity not exceeding 60%	• well ventilated	• ambient light	• heat/smoke detection • fire alarms • sprinkler system • extinguishers	• intruder resistant area • controlled access	• coated metal shelves	• accessible location • non-flood prone • non-polluted environment • bird, bat, insect and rodent proof	• robust, clean containers or boxes, • clean folders or envelopes
Paper (b) maps, plans, charts	• as above	• as above	• as above	• as above	• as above	• coated metal shelves or plan cabinets • rolled or vertical storage is acceptable	• adequate floor loading • pitched roof for water run-off	• robust, clean folders or containers
Photographic media black and white or colour, sheet film, cine film, x-rays, microforms, prints	• 20°C ± 2°C • 50% RH±5%	• as above	• as above	• as above	• as above	• coated metal shelves	• high capacity drainage system • no box gutters • loading dock separate from storage areas • cyclone proof	• robust, clean containers or boxes • clean folders or enclosures
Magnetic media computer tapes and disks, video tapes, audio tapes, magneto-optical disks	• as above	• as above	• as above	• as above	• as above	• non-magnetisable shelving		• non-magnetisable, sealed containers, cases or sleeves
Optical media compact and mini disks, laser disks	• as above	• as above	• as above	• as above	• as above	• coated metal shelves		• clean containers, envelopes or enclosures
Miscellaneous gramophone disks, models, objects, mixed media items	• temperature not exceeding 27°C • relative humidity not exceeding 60%	• as above	• as above	• as above	• as above	• as above		• clean containers, enclosures or wrapping

Index